Aster chilensis

or
Self-Immolation

Adam Baltieri

Prologue

Apparently I've elected myself to the editorship of a selection of my own writings. In other words, I must be interested in that practice of remaining whole: resting so peacefully in the brutality of change, with an immunity that would allow me to be pervaded by everything without forgetting who I am.

These writings seem to me the concretization of a reminiscence, an archaic memory, when life is made precarious by the love, the whims of an oblivious being: the tribulations of that crucible, in which the unbearable is born.

The ghost of what I once was, which always remains, wants to believe that I became what I am through her, yet this would be like holding onto myself. We all belong to being. I don't remember coming into being. I do not believe anyone remembers coming into being. However, since I remember remembering, I have dreamed of dying.

What is certain is that the following emails were written to someone. As editor, I have found it fitting to call her "Natalia," with its whisper of birth.

Aster chilensis is the botanical name for a flowering plant native to the west coast of North America. By way of adventitious explanation, it is something concrete and particular, rooting these words in life, history, and the earth. Throughout the years, my intentions were contained and grew under the header *Aster chilensis*. In fact, the small, star-like flower does not occur in Chile, as I found out in my researches: the plant was apparently misnamed.

I question whether I ever noticed the *Pacific aster* in the wild, and I no longer remember how it entered my world, becoming a fixed idea. My knowledge of the plant comes from the pictures and descriptions made available to me on the Internet. In the past, the name *Aster Chilensis* vaguely arose in my mind and stayed, with all the mystery of something arising from nothing. I began to believe that Natalia herself had told me about the flowers, although I have no evidence. My experience is not like recollection. The flower is simply there. It is like something known in a dream. I wondered what it was, this plant, this flower.

So it seems that a misnamed flower I've never seen has come to organize what is called my life, which otherwise has no outlines now.

It is fitting that something so circumstantial should become the signifier for my becoming. As anyone can attest, certain details become indelible. I have spent months, years, wondering where the name *Aster chilensis* came from, and all of a sudden I notice I have accomplished what seemed impossible: I can no longer distinguish the essential from the circumstantial. This is nothing more than a usual occurrence, something anyone is familiar with. It should alert us to the fact that we are moving within the whole. As editor bringing order into chaos I see it fit to make all kinds of proclamation. Life as we know it is the inexorable procession through which the whole becomes navigable. The irreducibility of an image, the California Aster, and its kinship with a mood—through which the bygone becomes accessible—is known, I presume, to anyone who has lived long enough.

There is always a demand to make sense, especially now as I write and edit these writings. Yet in my experience, when I have truly touched someone, it was beyond my understanding. It was life itself, and I have the suspicion that being has less to do with understanding than with a willingness to undergo experience. In other words, to choose to suffer: knowing full well we have no other choice.

In terms of what I am saying, it's as if I were a lunatic in a whirlwind of abstractions. I know, however, that I am one with everything that has happened.

So, to return to this Prologue that I'm writing: it now serves as a preface to emails I wrote to someone while experiencing. The Epilogue was written to you while I edited the emails.

I had premonitions that my experience was to become more than what I have become. In other words, I had great expectations concerning its transmutation in the communicable. In retrospect, it's as if I had planned my own demise.

However, I never planned to write these emails. They were written to a reality beyond me, whose truth I seldom glimpsed. And I never planned to edit a selection of my own writings, including these emails. While some may insist on the banality of such facts, others will notice that they are *not nothing*.

I suspect this history might bore you at times, may even seem silly. I am surprised that remembered desperation can take on characteristics of the comical. It all feels so gentle and human. Is this a sign of the ineffable wandering I am impelled to communicate?

These writings may require context in order to meet that demand to make sense. The circumstances concerning the origin of the emails are thus, as follows. A young student of philosophy, tempted by the promise of glimpsing into the heart of being, notices a young woman reading a book: she is sitting on a bench at the edge of campus. He walks past her, almost an entire city block, and turns around. I cannot remember what he said upon introducing himself to that young woman. The development is the cruelest of fates, wherein the tenderness of a boy's heart seeks refuge in the desperation of a girl who must break and dominate others in order to be able to need. The complimentary desperation of the lost young man, adrift on an unholy sea, tolerates well such cruel domination, as he is willing to give up everything

4

not to lose contact with the only thing keeping him in this world. Such exquisite sensitivity and fragility, the tenderness and receptivity of a newborn combined with the pretensions of a sage, must have appealed to someone living in a fortress who would not speak of herself. Thus, I continued to write to her, in her absence, according to her demands. I take it there is nothing unique here in the doggedness of my intention to exist. In one way, Natalia was absent simply because we studied at separate universities.

The letters arose at the time from the deepest source, which is to say from the factual, superficial circumstances of my life at the time. Over a decade later, I have begun to write again. I have lived with the unknown flower and the premonition that my experience was to be shared, although I have never known what I was going to say. That explains the Epilogue. While I've never known what I am going to say, this ignorance does not diminish the sense of who I am. It is rather a homecoming than its opposite: like coming home to a place you've never seen before.

I am experiencing the embarrassment of a skeptic to whom prophetic diction comes naturally. I know that I have only written of ordinary things, and in disclaiming them as such, I would like to avoid the surreptitious performance of something spectacular. Sometimes, speaking of the ineffable is like taking out the trash. Someone has to do it. I don't believe it is possible to force such visitations as I have known. And it is perhaps a sign of maturity to accept the banality of one's profoundest longing, one's purest deliverance.

The reader may wonder whether Natalia ever responded, may want to hear her voice. She never wrote to me. It is as if we spent an eternity together, and I believe she is responding to me all the time, which is another incredible thing to say, just like that the Absolute revealed itself to me in the name of a flower I've never seen. When I knew her, Natalia insisted that I write to her *always*, even—and perhaps especially—in her absence. I was loyal to her and hence to myself.

Supposing I never saw Natalia for who she was? Supposing I smothered her—if I may utter the pain of such violence—with my beleaguered, embattled imagination, just as I, for her, was sacrificed to the magical life-giving impossibility of *always*?

What if I never truly saw that girl sitting on the bench? What if she was only what I made her, even as I perceived her white blouse, leather sandals, her face and her hands? What if I effaced Natalia with my desperate hopefulness, as we in reciprocal isolation became entangled in lethal folly, leading me into the extreme latitudes of invisible suffering? I could not have been wholly alone.

Supposing I never truly knew Natalia, yet I am changed, what or who intervened?

What presence in these flames, in which I imagine my death? Who is responsible for the experience out of which I find myself building this pyre?

My love, I'm sorry for when I didn't see you. I would not have smothered you, had I known better. I just wanted to know you…

By way of providing more context for what in these writings doesn't make sense, the reader may know that Natalia is that moment when you are born in someone else's eyes, and now being, you know for the first time that the end is coming, and with a certain mute dignity, in that silence which is the birth of all conflagrations, you let go and die openly.

I cannot answer the question concerning the value of suffering. I know something of the unspeakable preciousness of being. Natalia touched my heart, and I found myself wondering what was beneath the mask I had confused for my face.

I have never been able to understand what I am, which I suppose is not unique, although it seems to be my peculiar preoccupation.

I found myself writing, and what has been written, has been written. Perhaps I am being a severe editor, certainly I am trying to do a good job. I suspect any deadness, abstraction is due to the intensity of a longing to be delivered from this world. At the same time, this longing was only born of a passion in this world and for this world. I was in love with Natalia and absolutely everything that has to do with her.

In editing these writings, I have for the moment exhausted my powers. I have, for the moment, had my fill of trying to understand what it is not possible for me to understand. The faintest outlines and what can be inferred must suffice. I believe these words must be love's ashes.

I do not understand what has been routinely demanded of me, including the editorship of these writings, along with their coy, paradoxical presentation, which has seemed befitting. It has not been an easy task, because I do not know why nor for whom I am editing. It may be one thing to make a sacrifice to God. Perhaps it is another to make a sacrifice to the Unknown. I question the worth of these invisible realms of suffering through which our lives take shape. And I know they have made me.

In the only language I've ever truly spoken: before I was born, I was to be.

And that which is called "chance" became "fate."

And that which was merely a matter of how you look at things, became everything.

And may the philosophers become experts in tautologies, as their lives unfold.

And may you consider this editorship a labor of love: a most peculiar blossoming, like a flower, before there were any.

Emails to Natalia

8/11/2008

When are you coming home?

I've been waiting patiently, but now I'm
deliberately losing composure.

Sorry for the e-mail. I was tempted to leave too
many messages on your phone, knowing that
it's probably not even with you anyway, but,
becoming uncomfortable with uncertainty—my
own failing—I thought you might get an email at
a stop along the road, and a word from you would
put me at rest.

Please call me or send a note if you can.

I remain very sincerely yours,
Adam B.

And for you my love,
the kiss on the lips shall never replace the kiss on
the cheek.Oh, let these giddy monarchs burst forth
from my navel!
But kill the caterpillars.

9

I only have a minute. I was prostrate on the bed upstairs in the house that my mom rented, when I felt like I would burst if I couldn't tell you something. It's such an awful feeling that I can't explain it.

I want to be a writer. I don't tell people that, because then I'd have to be one. There was a way that I thought I could describe the awful feeling in a book that I may write: A man seeks too ardently. He wants to observe sharks in the ocean, up close, safely from within the confines of a cage. But as he's watching the sharks, who beat their heads against the cage, the rope suspending the cage, tied to the side of the boat, breaks; and the cage begins to sink towards the bottom of the ocean. He can't leave the cage because of the sharks, but the cage is sinking into the cold, dark waters. The light at the ocean's surface begins to fade.

We went to some water falls today. Yesterday, I went window shopping downtown with my family. My sister sent me off to the philosophy section of a bookstore. I can't read books right now. I tried to explain to her how we know how long a second is, and how we know for sure what exactly one foot is. Do you know? I'd love to explain it to you if you don't. My family wasn't interested, and I missed the audience I usually have at your dining room table.

When I was younger I worried what would
happen if every ruler in the world disappeared:
what would happen to inches? I don't know why
I thought of it yesterday, but I read a book, maybe
a year ago, about relativity theory that explained
it. I'm pretty sure about this, but not completely—
that they used to keep a definitive ruler in a safe
somewhere in France. We don't do it that way
anymore.

I felt really horrible, buried amongst those
50,000 people, when we went to Golden Gate
Park together. I felt so uncomfortable and lost
when you walked away for such long intervals. I
wanted to steal you away... but then I was scared
of imposing myself; now I'm not so scared about
that sort of thing: life is an imposition.

Yours always,
Adam

9/26/2008

You're wonderful! You can't believe how vividly I
imagined you on your bike, making loops around
campus, standing up on the pedals in your high-
waist shorts!

I love hearing from you. I am so happy right now.

For one reason or another, I have become wary of
e-mail as a mode of communication. I wanted to
say more things, but I'll say them later.

11

9/27/2008

Dear my little dove, my dear,

It is imperative that you do everything
in your power to let me know that you are there,
even if you are not here. I write to you, so that
I allow you to participate in my life. I can't tell
you how perplexed and fearful I sometimes feel,
as my ability to be forever present directly in
my where and when deprives me of the security
of familiarity and the invisible reassurance of
thoughts reigned in by habit: as the very idea of
possibility is available to me, I can't recline in my
old idea of you, knowing that you're ever vital,
living away from me. I am always expecting.
It doesn't just come. This is the price of being
aware; and it seems impossible to me how anyone
who ever really loved anyone could tolerate being
apart from them.

Please write to me what happens to you,
and let me have what comes to you when you
write to me. You give me the greatest gift of all:
you let life happen, to me.

I guess that you sleep next to someone
else; but sleep next to me in your thoughts, even
if this is meager. Don't let your thoughts be about
me, but always to me, or for me. Don't ever say
"he" or "him" in your mind, when you think of
me, please! I don't know whether this is a silly

request, or what difference it makes, or fully what
I'm asking.

Don't ever become too comfortable. We are
young. And you have my heart. Don't let what
beats regularly slip into the background.

Yours,
Adam

9/28/2008

Dear Natalia,

I just read what I last sent to you, and I'll
say that I don't know exactly what it means.
Sometimes I have this terrible idea, and looking
at myself through that idea makes things seem
somehow pathetic. I mean this regarding means
of expression. I have this idea that an excess of
romanticism saves me from banality. But this back
and forth between myself and myself has gone
on for my entire life: when I was much younger
I'd accuse myself of assuming that I knew more
than other 7th graders, and then I'd accuse myself
of knowing nothing, of being conceited, and I'd
make all sorts of other claims about myself. It's
alright, it keeps me grounded.

Back to the point. I let idiotic philosophical
notions into what I say to you, when it is clear that
every human being—and not just the person who
makes it explicit—has experiences like these: the

13

strangeness of time, the strangeness of personality, the strangeness of love.

Now I want to address something you said. Even though everyone is awful, according to you, we speak their language. We are given the chance to speak because of them. But so that I'm not guilty of what I've just charged—being needlessly philosophical—, all I mean to say is that languages are living things, and if we had not grown into this language, it is certain that I would not even be able to be me for you, since I could not even tell you anything. Part of the problem is that this living source, this foundation for expression, is always found at the middle— and since we are so spread out, spread thin, if anyone wants to say anything meaningful they find themselves flying to vertiginous heights, an arduous effort not to fall down, to sustain that way of talking and seeing. And by the way, this is just more of that pretentiousness. I'd like to shake off intellectualism. The whole thing makes me feel like an idiot.

Back to the point again. For us to stay grounded, but above the common ground, and to real-ly interact is a gift.

To your health,
Adam

10/1/2008

Dear Natalia,

I'm leaving thoughts expressed in writing for
a few days, because that loss of everything has
caught up with me again, and I think it begins
when words make the world seem slippery in
comparison.

The thing is, is that, I want to speak to you
directly, those words which can never be captured
nor imitated, but slip away a moment after they're
said, sprung from our moment, lost by another.

It's so pleasing when you laugh about me. I'll say
the silliest things in the world for you.

Ardent care,
Adam

10/08/2008

Dear Natalia,

I'm sitting in the basement of the library trying
to finish an essay that I've put off writing for a
few weeks. I work down here because there is
nowhere to escape. Unfortunately, I can't know
if you're calling me because there is no cell
reception, but it's really important that I finish this
damn thing, which is somehow impossible, even
though I know exactly what I'm talking about
regarding the topic.

Is it bad, good, or just safe to not know what you
desire? I now understand the substance of what

I desire, but I have no idea how it will manifest
concretely. I have in mind such a long rest from
this way of life; not an abandonment, but a rest.
I'd like to work with my hands. Please let's paint.

Your,
Adam

10/12/2008

Dear Natalia,

You told me the cops pulled you over and
discovered contraband. You alluded to a night in
prison, but I haven't heard from you since.

This is for no other reason than that it will warm
you to know that I imagine you sleeping on a cot
in a prison cell. I wonder if they put you in a cell
all alone, or if you are in a cell with another. I
wonder if they will give you paper, and if they do,
will you write down what happened so that I will
know you better when you return.

The other thing you should know is, I don't
really think you're in prison, but I am concerned
because I haven't heard from you.

This is just because I want to make you feel good:
you now know yourself in my imagination, in a
cell, alone, in prison.

Does it please you to know that I remember
pomegranate seeds and your fingers?

Tenderly,
Adam

10/30/2008

Natalia,

Most important: remember to laugh cheerfully
with me about things like this at a later time.

There is a certain concentration of mind that
brings about something original when diverted
into words, and it is this originality that assures
of presence. There is sureness in knowledge that
words came from another creativity.

Yours doggedly,
Adam

11/1/2008

I'll try not to be needlessly literary, though you
should know it isn't an effort to be so.

What I want to say is very simple; it might get lost
in the complexity of these sentences.

I want to know if you've watched over any
children. I'd like for you to let me hear you speak
Russian. I want to gossip pettily with you about
girls wearing racy underwear and carrying police
batons on Halloween.

This is my imagination: you try to say something,
but it's like the wind is knocked out of you and
the words don't come, only it isn't painful.

How sad would it be if I were in my room relating
myself toward my imagination? That is why you
need to speak clearly. Please summon up yourself,
after you wake this morning from festivities at
which you either had a good time: life lived itself
and delivered you from this; or at which you were
the observer. Summon up something. Run through
the rain if you need to get away and call me from
under the cover of some dripping tree.

It is raining so profusely and the wind is battering
the windows.

Keep this in mind while you ponder: certainty
in the present cannot be wholly derived from the
past; the past can only shed diffuse light on the
future; and when something new comes it cannot
be explained by its parts.

Oh yes, the simple point: I want to know if
you've babysat, if it's raining, what you did for
Halloween, whether or not you have to do chores.

No—really what I need is simple confirmation,
even if in the form of resistance, to end the
psychological debilitation of suspense.

Yours sadly,
Adam

11/7/2008

Natalia,

I have not gotten my point across.

You don't understand what you do when you stop communicating. I assume this. Do you understand the simplicity of my words?

You are being cruel.

Your cruelty is the power of arbitrariness. (I don't know when it's going to happen; I don't know why it's going to happen; I don't know when it's going to end.)

Are you teaching me a lesson? If that is what you're doing I swear solemnly that I understand. I swear to you one hundred times in contrition that I understand. I throw myself at your feet.

Yours as always,
Adam

11/26/2008

Dear Natalia,

I wonder if you'll ever forgive me for being too serious at times, but within your forgiveness recognize seriousness without being too serious.

19

I mean this sincerely, from a healthy balance
regained.

Do you understand the contradictions that I send
to you?

I have to tell you that as these notes accumulate,
pile up, I begin to feel sheepish about sending
more of them, thinking of all the past thoughts not
thought through, though lived, that I've sent to
you.

I feel off balance, awkward, like I might fall over.

The reason, I think, is that I haven't yet recovered,
begun anew, since when I sat in your dark sun
room, alone, listening to you weeping, after you
told me to turn off my light, emphasizing that it
was my light, waiting for you, not feeling like it
was given to me to comfort you, overcome by
helplessness.

Feeling this way shows me to myself what you
mean.

On the other hand, I've never felt closer to you
than I do now, and in a very strange way I savor
what happened, as something very painful, but
precious between us. Something very serious and
precious that brought me very close to you.

Besides all these other things, I wanted you to
know something very important. I hope to do
well with my life, for I want to be around healthy
people whom I can love, and whose love I

deserve, and who can see what I do. But I do not
want to ask for too much.

I have to take a break so that I can get lots of
practical things in line, since I'm graduating and
so on.

I don't think that this should happen, but I don't
want you to be disappointed if I can't be crazy all
the time—I say this with a laugh, but you know
what I mean. I'm smiling at you, by the way.

With love,
Adam

12/4/2008

Dear Natalia,

I think about your daily life and that I cannot
know it. Sometimes, when I am irrationally, and
therefore completely, convinced that everything
is all wrong with the way we—signifying the
greater "we"—live, it becomes unendurable and
impossible that we should be apart in this simple
way. I become very worried about life. But when
I am more sober this feeling resolves itself into a
mild sadness.

I once thought that to disclose oneself in words
was somehow the highest way to be close.

I now understand a different way. The most
contrastive way to explain what I mean is to say

that I am in this other way closest to you when
we are sleeping. It's not that I am sleeping, and
you are sleeping, and we happen to be near one
another. No, we sleep, together, and we enter into
one another.
It is this same way to closeness that is being
with you in an everyday way, everyday. It is an
ineffable comfort, a wordless craving.

The other way is more austere, with words, and it
is coldly independent. It is about a different part
of the soul.

I want both.

But now I want you to fall asleep with me.

12/5/2008

Dear Natalia,

I spent this morning reading in bed. I've started
the book of source material for modern art theory
that your mom gave me. I read parts of Van
Gogh's letters from the 1880s.

This stuck out, and though it is a more or less
common theme—I think—it is really something
to experience for oneself.

He writes in a letter to his brother, "... my only
anxiety is, how can I be of use in the world? Can't
I serve some purpose and be of any good?"

This is a very complex question, as it seems that
upon serious and genuine reflection the tenets of
safe, traditional moral systems break down in the
face of life to be frighteningly exposed in all their
superficiality. This does not mean that hope is lost;
but rather it frees one's attention for our moments
and gives opportunities to relate genuinely to
the reality of present situations, which does not
usually entail a rote morality.

Nevertheless, being overwhelmed this morning, a
thought came to my mind in the form of a vague
hope for the future that mollified me and freed me
to go about my day, which was all the more in the
sense that I can share it with you.

In particular, I thought about what you said about
Monet in the print shop, that he spent so much
time studying and getting everything just right
and that it is a worthy thing to do. Your beholding
and understanding a thing like that leaves me
feeling reassured somehow, especially in that you
revealed it to me. It is somehow a little evidence
of your being that makes me feel safe in my own
striving.

12/10/2008

I just wanted to hear your voice.

I know that nothing significant could have been
said, but I just wanted to hear your voice.

I call you day after day to let you know that I need
to hear your voice, because even action made
ridiculous can mean more than the things that
mean things in the first place: words.

You are conspicuously missing. I don't even dare
to begin to think why, which would have me
worrying about you for such stupid reasons. Yet,
I allow myself to worry because I don't like the
peacefulness of fatalism: that I won't be able to
hear from you until you speak.

Stifled by such pressing pressure, when all that
I spontaneously will must be caught and added
to that pressure, I dream of you and me in an
open field. I dream of you screaming at me and
me shouting at you, of kicking and pounding at
the earth. I dream about a ferocious anger gifted
safely to me;

Besides this sublimation, without the complexity
of abnormal sentences, I am hurting. Why don't
you say, "Hello?" I mean it.

Adam

12/10/2008

The calamity for me is being left in the dark. Have
you ever walked through your home when it is
pitch black, and the night comes to you cleanly?
You walk unafraid, familiar with your own home.
But for a moment, maybe, before you reach
the threshold of a door, you fall backwards and

forwards in your own mind, and grope for the
walls that would lead you surely to an exit. I am
prone to this swaying that arrests in its confused
motion in the times that you keep me in the dark.
But only for a moment, then I'm once again I am
surely in my home.

Turn on the lights when you can. I don't
understand right now.

Yours always,
Adam

12/14/2008

I feel as if you were shutting me out.

It is painful. There is an "as if."

My head is so heavy with ideas and questions,
seldom do any of them enter the clarity of
consciousness.

What if I am exhausted and broken? What if I
have so many dirty dishes in my sink and my
room is upset like my mind?

I cut my finger on a broken tea cup last night. I
stood frightened and still before the blood came.
My hands were wet with soap and water, so when
the blood came it poured down my thumb and
down the side of the sink, when I turned off the
water. I was full of fear. It hadn't yet begun to
hurt, and I was staring at it. In front of the dark

window at the sink, I was so scared of what was
going to happen, that it couldn't happen. I told
myself it wouldn't hurt very much—it was just
a cut. The anticipation hurt me. I tremulously
peeled back the skin to make sure it wasn't too
deep. It didn't hurt very much. The blood came.

It is almost healed this morning, and caused me
no trouble in sleep.

With my eyes closed, I whisper: Where are you?
Where are you?

There is too much fog. Why won't the sun come
out? My room is so cold. I am confined to my bed.

Well, I'll stumble around today, too; write a
philosophy paper that asks me to use the deepest
part of myself, which I cannot use right now.

12/17/2008

Dearest Natalia,

It is important right now that you let me know that
you care about me. I know, with a strong sense,
that it might be wrong for me to ask, for so many
reasons.

I try to hold onto you as the last time that I saw
you or heard you, but it is very hard. I know that
you continue to live and experience. I know that
you live away from me, but in a stronger sense
that you live in another world. At once I want to

know that world completely and feel that it isn't
right for me to know it, that it is wrong of me, that
there is nothing to gain.
As I've tried to say to you in so many ways, it
is this floundering hopelessness in the dark that
wrecks me.

You remain mysterious to me, but the pain that
this sometimes causes me feels right. I mean that
I don't see how it could be any other way, and this
'mystery' as I've called it—this strange mixture
of hardness and softness, austerity, sensitivity of
your soul—is what I need. But it is very hard
when my desire to know you is frustrated, because
you do not show yourself often.

With care,
Adam

12/18/2008

I just remembered your hand in my hand at the
clinic, and the warmth of your stomach.

I'm going to lay off the emails after this, unless
you tell me otherwise, because I don't want them
to be a vexation.

Did you coo and yawn and stretch for someone
else this morning!

Well, I can suspend myself and my thoughts in
the fragrant intoxication of a flower bud until you
return.

Find me,
Adam

Dear Natalia,

I need to figure out whether hope on a large scale
is delusional. There's got to be a way to hope with
some sort of humility.

I know that if I only concern myself with my
small life and the people that I care about
immediately, that I'm permitted more hope than
most people I know.

On the other hand, it feels black-hearted to believe
that martyrs are insane—say, some revolutionary
who was put in prison, who wrote a giant
political-economic manifesto that now has the
aura of a bible—and that the people who look up
to them are equally deluded.

But you know, this caring about one's own life
and the people that one loves is the very solution
that I have to offer, supposing anyone was
looking for a solution—but its really extremely
complicated, even though it sounds simple.

More or less pining for you,
Adam

12/24/2008

Dear soul, my heart,

If it is even possible, you must explain to me
in the future where it was that you dwelt inside
yourself during these times, or it will remain a
perplexing mystery to me.

But I know that I shouldn't expect that to be
possible.

I would silently accept the miracle of your faith
in me, as you have miraculously accepted mine
in you. I am overwhelmed by your way of being.
Your thoughts are what I need and want, but I
believe that I know them, and I believe that I
know why I can't know them from you, and if I
am right about it, then I am stunned by your grace.

I realize that to have faith in the purest sense is to
be a fool from the outside, but I think that it is one
of the most beautiful things. It is only when I see
myself from the outside that I sometimes falter in
mind.

Faithfully,
Adam

12/25/2008

In my imagination I hear your voice harmonizing
with the steaming tea kettle that belongs so

completely to your home, and I miss you on this
Christmas.

12/28/2008

Dear Natalia,

Nothing comes to me spontaneously tonight, so
that if I were to write anything special to you, it
would be contrived, even if it did sound like me.
Yet, I want to imagine you're reading this email,
and I want you to know that you are in my
thoughts.

If it weren't for the sureness of electronic
transmission, I would have to assume that all my
notes are lost when I send them.
It is psychologically difficult, strange, not
to receive confirmation: consciousness must
keep natural inclination in check, which wants
to feel like you don't get my notes; and, in this
case, I can truly say that you live in me, as my
imagination must create you as you change when
you read my notes, which change I cannot know
in actuality.

This sometimes makes me feel confused,
forgetful, blind. It is only due to the care with
which I attend to you. When we are apart, it is
probably best that I forget about you, rather than
spread my attention thin. But that is something I
would rather not do.

I suppose I had more to say than I thought I did.

This all only means that I am in need of a long,
long, intimate conversation with you.

Don't worry if you can help it. I keep writing
about things that needn't be said only because I
want you to have more to read.

Goodnight,
Adam

12/29/2008

Natalia,

I feel rested after so many easy days at home.
I can't think of anything to do tonight. I am
bored and restless, and I wish that I could think
of something worthwhile to do. I brought some
books with me, but I can't bring myself to read
them right now: a long book about the causes of
the second world war, theories about the end of
history, the loss of shared values, the difference
between humans and animals, history of
philosophy, the end of poetry and so on.
My parents' house is still under construction. My
room is as you saw it, but the bed is in the corner
now for some reason.

You know, in a way, you give me the strength to
be what I am, admonishing me for time wasted,
for entertaining bad company.

31

Someone always compliments me on the coat,
wherever I go. I feel good wearing it. It is also a
source of strength, coming from your closet, that
allows me to be what I am.

I'd like to return your gloves to you soon, so that
we can go out together with them.

Crossing the bridge the other day into the city, I
imagined it falling into the bay, the horror of all
the cars and people and broken cement sinking
in confusion through the debris-laden water. I
remember feeling upset and disappointed, because
there was somewhere that I wanted to go and
there was a life that I wanted to live.

Call me when you can.

Your,
Adam

12/29/2008

My dear heart,

I cannot sleep. I feel as if I might go mad. The
cosmic perspective that I try to retain, especially
in times of anxiety, will ensure that I do not;
but it is very important that you know that I at
least could go mad for want of your thoughts.

I would pronounce my faith and my love for
you over and over and over if I weren't afraid
of wearing out my pronouncements or, worse
yet, appearing blind and unreasonable. I would

express it in as many intemperate ways as I could
imagine, if it weren't for my concern to let you
know the solidity and reality of my love—for I
may demand much from me and you, but my love
and hope are still of the earth.

I want us to be, I need us to be, completely
transparent to each other, even if it is painful,
which isn't to say that it would be: but I want you
to know the sincerity of my desire. I can therefore
only exhort you to let me know your thoughts.

I need you now, because I miss you, and I can't
think very well anymore: I can only poorly guess
as to how you feel right now, and this state leaves
me confused and sometimes embarrassed.
I don't know how much more I can endure.

I love you,
Adam

12/30/2008

I am coming home soon.

Say, at least, hello, for I am mentally exhausted,
broken, and listless. It's ridiculous to call a whole
bunch, because you won't let me talk to you—or
can't talk to me—until you do talk to me. I could
hold out for a long time, but now I'm having
trouble.

I'm worried about sounding dramatic, but there is
just no way to explain this to you. I ask honestly

for you to relieve me, for I am in pain, my head is
so tired.

Yours with such sincerity,
Adam

12/30/2008

My problem is very straightforward, so
straightforward it's silly: missing you while
not being able to see you, and coping with
uncertainty. An example of the latter. I don't even
know whether you've read the previous emails I
sent. Obviously, I have reason to believe that you
have, but practically it is like sending missives
into a cold void. After so many days without any
sort of confirmation, the effect is amplified into
an unavoidable loneliness. It is so disheartening,
I don't know whether you understand.
Nevertheless, I instinctively have things to tell
you. I usually hope for joy in response to what I
write, but which I will never be able to genuinely
know.

Your gloves in my car are comforting.

Really, and truly,
Adam

Dear N,

I wrote the following sentences to you this morning.

Last night you said to me, "I am tired and— what's the word?—disillusioned." When you said it, I felt something slipping away, and a sense of futility set in. But then I resolved to "not let you" be disillusioned.

I stumbled through reading a letter to you as you fell asleep, pressing ahead with a ridiculous confidence, trying to make the moment what it wasn't, trying to assert an urgency that wasn't there.

"Sometimes, we can sit together, we don't always have to talk."—or, you said, "I don't always have to talk."

I continued onward, trying to stifle all embarrassment at reading to you inchoate thoughts, putting faith in words, hoping like a performer that in just another moment I could show you something spectacular, but the moment never came; the words remained dumb.

I sit here this morning demanding of the world in general—"I know there was something special about this! I know there was something extraordinary that animated my words!" Yet it is like trying to excite someone to a momentary, unimportant thrill, while all they can do is be normally.

Well, here, then, come the truest moments.

Disillusion: "The disappointing loss of a belief or an ideal." (To lay it out so clearly makes me wince and then ache.)

I don't know in what sense this has happened.

"It is our responsibility to return vividness to the mundane." Is that something I said?

It's also true that in life many things are needed— but what does that mean?

It might be wise not to write when words are dead. I can't help it.

However, I am not worried, although I remain, and will remain, concerned—nothing having to do with you will ever stop being important. I hope to say truly that I have had no illusions; and that therefore lulls in general—in writing, in relating, in being, in you—are parts foreseen in a meaningful whole to be actively cultivated. There are enormous explosions on the sun, hurtling light and life towards the earth all the time, but the sun sets every day, and few people even watch it. "The terrible thing about beauty is that we can become accustomed to it, and that is why winter is valuable."—well, many allowances must be made to derive the proper meaning from that; allow its

pretension to solace—also ignore, for the moment,
the sublimity of the cold, the desolate.

Aha! You see how clever I am! (Now I make fun
of myself...) The sun's great, chaotic explosions
never cease, yet the sun must and does become
familiar, must become part of the background,
almost completely ignored as a condition for
the support of other things: such as—paying
a parking ticket! Likewise, my love, while the
extraordinariness may recede to the background
to allow for other things, the small acts that string
together a life, it never really leaves.
The extraordinariness is always present,
but so often feels like illusion when the world
normalizes—but which to awakened thought
is always the ceaseless reality; this will never
leave—it only must recede to make way for the
immediacy of life and our slow, tacit complicity,
from the new to the old, from the surprising to the
commonplace.

We live in this tension, and that is how I would
understand your disillusionment: not as a loss,
but as the necessary vacillation between losing
and regaining, as that necessary movement
between being astonished by the brilliancy of
the sun, and not noticing it while it continues to
light the commonplace as one sleeps in the shade,
dreaming of other things.

I therefore hope to share in your disillusionment,
to fall asleep with you in a normal bed, to
confront well practical needs—to not lose sight of
the whole; in keeping with the whole I hope that

all moments will validate themselves—at least
that is what I must believe.

Adam

1/21/2009

Dear Natalia,

The world is unfamiliar and I feel displaced. I
was joyful almost all day long, but after a while I
couldn't keep it up for lack of familiar reciprocity;
now a certain loathing has set in. Things are
overwhelmingly and reassuringly simple. I mean
things at large, though there is always a doubt
about it—the simplicity, I mean. Peeing on the
side of the road, one wonders. It's good to do
it with someone, the wondering I mean—the
peeing, too. I'm scared to settle into my mind
after so much activity. The metaphors we use to
explain the inexplicable to one another will never
be replaced by something more rational. I don't
mean about anything special. Describe any setting
or scene: those are the words inexplicably clear.
When you tell me you understand, I believe you.
That's very good and worthy. My fondness for
you grows quite a bit. Thankfulness is wistful and
afraid, for it understands that which is here may
go. That goes for most things. How can I say my
thanks?

Adam

38

1/23/2009

Dear Natalia,

I just left the discussion group for my history class, and now I feel so disheartened that it is hard to go about my day. There are many reasons for this: the inauthenticity of the student instructor, confusions about how it is possible to figure out history at all, annoyance that in every class I go to they should stress the fact that "all points of view are biased, it is impossible to be objective"— which may be true, but if it is true it is a truism; that is to say, it is old news, and I can't understand what emphasizing it does when human thinkers have been dealing with it for too many years to count. There is something deep about saying so— believe it or not—,but it is very hard to bring this out for a student, and the rote repetition of this relativism trope leads to very shallow thinking and a sort of tacit excuse not to be engaged or to make decisions about anything. The world is debilitated by uncertainty.

1/25/2009

Dear Natalia,

I was about to write you a letter which, with hope in its words, would explain how and why we did not find each other last night.

Instead, I will only ask you—not to forgive me for wanting to console you—but for feeling

that I needed to console you, that I should have
been able to console you, which feeling caused
my failure. In my heart I would gladly accept
such a responsibility, but we both know what
independence requires, even if love wants to
overcome it.

Have faith that I did not mistake you, for if I did
not respond well, it is only because I lay in my
bed in mute terror, not knowing what to do.

Your tears are my consolation.

1/26/2009

Dear Natalia,

I have a moment, so I'll write a note. Taking only
one philosophy class this semester, I feel as if I
were in high school again. Actually, even worse,
and strangely, a feeling of forlornness that I
remember has come back to me. I used to ride the
bus to school every morning, listening to really
bad music in my headphones. I can't really put
into the words those juvenile feelings of isolation
and withdrawal.

I want to say sorry for being dramatic last night.
For various reasons it is horrible to talk on the
phone—especially when we cannot hear each
other, bad reception. And writing to you has has
gotten complicated in a very small, unimportant
way, as follows. It is much better to express what
I will call a more or less timeless sentiment in

writing, than to write about daily concerns, which
are in a way rather more complicated.

I will certainly, as they say, 'get over it', but I
can't stand to think that for even a moment you
felt bad—for lack of a more specific language
to describe it—due to a misinterpretation of my
words.

I think at certain times it is much more important
that you see my face than hear me say anything,
and much more important for me to see your face
than to hear you say anything. Yet, that isn't
possible sometimes, and we will cope. Would it
even be possible to exaggerate the importance of
the face? I think it is impossible. And certainly the
adjective "faceless", which is used to describe so
many aspects of contemporary life, ought to be
given much more gravity than it is. It is, I think,
the gravest adjective we know.

I have been feeling out of sorts, scattered is the
right word. I give almost no attention to my
schoolwork. I don't even feel like I am forgetting
something, I just don't think about it. As if I didn't
even have homework. But I do. I understand what
you mean when you say that if you took more
than three classes you would just forget what
you're taking. As I said, it isn't even a matter of
fighting forgetfulness, but it is forgetting about
forgetting. At least, that's what I'm experiencing.

In your daily instability and capriciousness, I am
stabilized. You are a ground for me, but I do try
not to put too much weight on you.

I am going to German class. It is important
sometimes to remember certain moments in the
past. It is not important to say which, because
memory has its own way of highlighting. Such
moments bring clarity to the present, for me.

Adam

1/26/2009

Dearest Natalia,

There are many things that I have thought to say.
I will avoid all of them. They are unimportant. I
hope to find that which underlies. In their stead I
say only this: trust me. That's all there is to say.

Do not take it as an insult or hold it against me if
I should assume in my heart that everything is a
misunderstanding. If it isn't, be brave enough to
show me. If it might be, be honest enough so that
we may know each other.

If you need to ask yourself questions, ask good
ones, and answer honestly. If you need to find
something out about me, ask me.

If I didn't think that your detestation of necessity
were due to something deeper, then I would gladly
call you childish.

Trust me. Or at least willfully test me, and then
detest me if I am not worthy of your trust.

And please, be more courteous—I mean in an
everyday way.

With love,
Adam

Dear Natalia,

It is sunny in Berkeley. I am wearing my light
blue shirt which smells of sun lotion and the
beach.
It is warm, but the wind is cool. I have my sleeves
rolled up and I'm flipping a quarter into the wind
and catching it in my palm as I walk through the
crowds of students, carrying loosely my lunch bag
in my other hand.
I hoped to see you walking towards me today.

Adam

Dear Natalia,

Is there some point at which words become
tiresome? When one becomes tired.

I worry because you worry: I worry how to
alleviate your worries.

I also worry because you worry about worrying me. This makes me worry that you won't tell me things straight.

There are many reasons for worry.

I also worry that I worry without reason.

Sometimes I do not worry at all. But then I worry because I think I should worry more.

There is a lack of stability in our relationship that we may secretly savor. Oh... yes, I'll say sorry for speaking for you.

However, I think it is right to worry in general—rather, to have concern.

Try your best. Chin up. Don't stop now.

I am the one who writes. You are the one who reads. I am the one who asks. You are the one who listens. I am the one who guesses.

Do you want to spend half your time in San Francisco, half your time in Paris?

Do you want to comb my hair? I would like to comb yours.

Were you born as you were, complete, at age 19, on a bench?

Did you order a peppered drink which your throat rejected at age 21?

Did you awkwardly lumber at the edge of a lake?
No, I find your legs and feet most graceful. I am
satisfied by your self-satisfaction when, lying on
your back on your bed, you watch your own legs
peddle through the air.

Is it true that you spend a good deal of time
thinking about colors? I heard that you like brown
paper bags.

Are you often late?

Is it true that hiding truth is to your advantage?

I sleep in an apartment in a bedroom above the
street between blue and brown sheets.

Adam

1/30/2009

Also, imagine me making faces at myself in the
mirror.

I miss you.

Adam

2/1/2009

Dear Natalia,

I wish that you would call me. I had this terrible
feeling on Friday night: I really wanted to know
what you were doing. For the sake of knowing
what you were doing, not for knowing what in
fact you were doing.

That you will read my words but I can't reach you
by phone feels arbitrary, and makes me sad. A tiny
bit of helplessness, even if almost nothing, is still
awful.

I'm doing my homework at your house today.

In your room, looking out the window over the
trees in the yard, I felt so happy.

Time will always tell, but instead of waiting
vexedly for the telling, now I feel as if time were
on my side: that it is my assurance, a guarantor. I
feel that even in the worst case time will not have
failed me, simply because it can't but tell.

What are you doing over there in your self? Over
distances you would withdraw completely, and in
my presence you would shroud yourself in joy.

Look outside, spring is coming. I don't know how
you are, but be calm. Calm yourself. This is good
advice regardless of circumstance.

Feel your head against a pillow, soft white linen.
I am here to run my hands through your hair. Just
let me, don't worry so much about it.

Adam

2/1/2009

The other thing is that I'd just like to say hello to you—in other words, we needn't really "get into anything."

I'm only protesting because I miss you.

Would you kindly put the foam from a cappuccino in my beard or something?

2/11/2009

Dear Natalia,

To focus all of one's attention on that which surrounds us, a room, the atmosphere of a room, the sky as perimeter, everything comprehended by the horizon, is to know each thing and to own each movement. Yet, one must not become shortsighted. I see the way that my hands move as I type this to you, and feel my fingers against the keys, so that most of what I am is in my fingers and the keys; and while doing so it seems impossible to understand how these movements should in sum produce a sentence. Likewise, focusing all of one's attention on the day—the day is what one does during the day, how one feels during the day, what the day brings us and what it takes away from us—it seems difficult to understand how all of the days should in sum produce a life.

One must master the ability to be both here and away at the same time. This mastery entails detracting nothing from the day while remaining aware of the life: not to get caught up in and confused by the intricacy of the day, but not to fall into the abyss of largeness that is life as it expands incomprehensibly in time in our imaginations.

I mention this to you now because I don't want the sometimes abrupt contrast between my intensity and sobriety to unnerve you, to vex you, to worry you. In times of aloofness, I am only pulling myself together, tying loose ends, reestablishing the balance between the large and the small, marrying feelings with thoughtfulness. This is necessary, and I want you to feel secure enough in my care so that you will not worry. I am still with you—I am preparing myself to remain with you. Let me be aloof by your side, do not worry. I need it, and it isn't anything to fret about when I go back inside myself. It may even feel like indifference. It is not.

Love,
Adam

2/17/2009

Dearest Natalia,

You know: I won't stop writing to you.

Outside the thunder is cracking while Strawberry
Creek rages pleasantly by.

I want you to know that, besides everything else,
I intend to be reliable, no matter what. Emphasize
"no matter what" so that its literal signification
comes to the front: admitting multiple
possibilities, but pledging reliability through them
all. To put it another way, I will never disappear: I
will always be either here or there. But you know
where I intend to be.

Oh pleasant thunder!

Adam

3/9/2009

I was resting on the grass under a tree, whose pink
and white flowers you reveal to me. I picked up a
petal and held it above my face. It was illuminated
and ethereal. Its edges blended softly with the
sky. Curled into my arm, I closed my eyes. I was
outside for a long time.

I worried about you. I wanted to know that you
are alright.

I worried that the stillness of the grasses would
take your will as mine was taken today.

I need to write and think, but my mind is too still.
I have historical facts to memorize, but my mind
is too still.

I had a daydream this morning about happiness,
while I washed the dishes. The circumstances
were very simple. We decorated a space together.
The weather was warm. We sometimes had people
for tea. I always wore light colors and comfortable
shirts whose collars you turned up.

I saw a movie last night. It was French. And the
clothes they wore were beautiful. Yet, the family
was working class.

Do you feel the world encroaches on your light
feelings? The colors on one's dress need burn so
brightly to hold back the darkness. May I walk in
the halo of your light?

Your,
Adam

3/17/2009

Dear Natalia,

Your fingers... Oh, how can I really describe it?
When I saw them resting on the table, maybe
on a sheet of paper, I felt deeply satisfied. The
strangeness of being, the hopelessness of ever
understanding, helped me to understand, and only
made your fingers more precious to me. We have
much to talk about. I know you will be brave as I
will try to be.

Exhaustion prevails, and so the body has a little triumph over the spirit. We can talk when we both have energy.

Adam

3/18/2009

Dear Natalia,

I very much wish that we had time and space in which to talk. I wish now to spend a long, meditative, but casual day with you, so that we might talk a little over breakfast, be by ourselves—intermittently you with yourself and me with mine—on the beach for a while in the afternoon, in the same room with each other in the evening, gathering ourselves over tea, while I do something and you do something, and then to come to closeness at night, whispering in bed our understanding. Throughout this week I feel exposed and hurried without my confidant.

Stay "in touch."

Love,
Adam

3/21/2009

Natalia, dearest to me, ineffable existence somehow still grounded in a body that is at the moment too far away from me—

51

Dear one,

I miss you very much. I long to communicate with you without words, to fall back into your rhythm, to conspire with you: to construct that foundation upon which our words will be given their proper weight. The facts do not justify my feelings right now—I feel like a chaos has swept between us.

3/23/2009

Dear heart,

I won't waste any time at all tallying up the facts and figures—irrelevant, impertinent.

One might deem meeting indifference with care as being pathetic. It isn't. I hope that soon you will know and feel the familiar faith. I hope that you won't stubbornly refuse my hand offered to you.

I fear that your feet aren't even ticklish right now. Let me breathe into you! Wake up! Wake up!

Yes, I understand you. I understand. But you should be more direct and spare my momentary heart.

I imagine a large corner of a bed sheet thrown back, and I miss you: awaiting the heaviness of your head.

3/23/2009

I was sitting on the couch in your living room,
reading a book, and I became bewildered by
words. Completely bewildered and frightened by
the way that words shape our lives.

Silence.

Deep in meditation on you, a mild warmth,
perplexity—how can I know how you receive
what I send?

Where do we exist during time spent out of sight?

And there you are, inexplicable.

Goodnight Natalia, I don't mean to be too grave,

Adam

3/27/2009

Dear Natalia,

Our talks before sleep are remembered liked
a dream; and, like a dream, disparate things
flow together coherently, but the principle
which coheres them confusingly eludes me like
something meaningful.

I will pay for half the cost of developing our film,
if you let me.

Adam

53

4/4/2009

Dear Natalia,

I am in your home. Your mom sounds tired. I worried about coming, but now I am here. I will sleep in your sun room tonight soundly.

I don't know if you understand. Because of your sometimes loss of contact, I start to feel lost. I don't know where my words are going.
Instead of dialoguing, I begin to feel like I am monologuing. And I start to feel exposed and vulnerable. Left on its own this doesn't make a whole lot of sense.

You are uniquely unpredictable. Sometimes you ask why I do not call. Other times I cannot reach you.

Once you were frightened because I hide nothing of myself. I become frightened in your darkness.

All that I know how to do and all that I know is right is to continue to be brave. Sometimes, I falter. I falter and then plunge: I wonder if I am not brave but foolhardy, and I become embarrassed.

I wish you would talk to me as the friend you have always hoped I would be, that you feared you might lose. Most of the time I understand small things without you telling me. But if you told me, I would feel recognized, looked in the eyes.

And a misunderstanding should be cleared up. I
want always for us to have an understanding, but
even if we have an understanding, that doesn't
mean we always understand each other.

You remain my little dove,
Adam

4/5/2009

Dear Natalia,

I wrote to you last night feeling satisfied.

Then I awoke feeling so serious. Too serious. I
want to chastise myself for being serious.

I want to be twenty-one. I want to be young. (That
means perfectly what it means to us in our times.)

I am not going anywhere. That doesn't here
mean: I won't budge. It means, there is time.
There is so much time.

I don't feel like working. I don't want to think.
Spring pulls at me. I miss your body. I am still
feeling under the weather.

I thought there was more I wanted to say. I don't
like being frightened of shadows, of stabbing at
phantoms. The intensity of your presence is born
out by a fickleness that is sometimes cruel.

55

Isn't it natural for me to wonder: What the hell is
Natalia doing? What is she thinking right now?

Your,
Adam

There are many birds calling to each other
behind your mom's house. It is always beautiful
through your window. The glass through which
I look: your bed, your curios, your records, your
thoughts, your heart, your body, your feet, your
gown, your smell, your laugh, your scamper, your
coo, your bed, your shoes.

4/6/2009

Dear Natalia,

I cannot explain to you how much grief you are
causing me by not just calling.

I have to resort to almost hilarious analogies to
have you understand this.

Suppose I fell into a booby-trap and I am now
stuck in a deep, dark pit. Your call would be like
magic: I would disappear and materialize above
ground.
Suppose you were a friend in a high place. I was
wrongly accused of something and sentenced
to death. If you said a few words to the judge, I
would get off. And in this case, you know I'm
innocent.

Suppose I were severely dehydrated, so that
not only was I in great pain but at great risk of
expiring. You have water. If you would only give
me one sip, I'd be alright.

I use hyperbole not to stress the reality of
the situation, but only to express to you
my exasperation. The analogies are important,
because in each case what needs to be done to
save me is so easy, that even a stranger would do
it.

In the ridiculous analogies, in each case
something trivial kept you from the phone, and I
subsequently died three times unnecessarily.

Will you please, please, please, please, please call
me. Please.

Adam

4/8/2009

My dear Natalia,

I love you and only you. I cherish you as a
complete being.

We are separated and I continue to relate to you as
if you were in my midst. This is a problem. You
wonder sometimes about what I do when you are
not here. I wonder often about what you do when
I am not there.

(Think about what I mean about the sureness of
the body, and now think about the meaning the
idiom "to keep in touch.")

Words are bothersome because they want to be
interpreted. And being apart from each other
creates a gap in our interpretations. This makes
uneasiness. The gap is closed the moment I set
eyes on you.

I have to be brave enough not to worry that
everything behind me will disappear. This is a
general worry I have.

Remember the thing about words and
interpretations and the gap. I'll see you soon.

Love,
Adam

4/15/2009

Dear Natalia,

There is something important that I want to ask
you to do. Would you write out a story for your
life: what you care about, how you want to live,
and what you hope for? It does not have to be
very specific, but if you have very particular
things in mind, I would like for you to write those
things too. It can be as elaborate or as simple as
it needs to be: the only thing that matters is to
do it in such a way that it will flow freely from
you. It is important to feel the weight of reality

58

throughout, but by this I don't mean to imply that 'reality' admits only mundane pathways nor that it should weigh on you in a 'stressful' way. I do mean that you should keep in mind the practical difficulties of moving around in this world full of so many people. I want you to keep all of these things in mind only for the integrity of my request and your response, since we can only really mean to do what can be done in a world where we are limited as we are.

There is nothing that is more important to me right now than that I know these things from you. I feel whole and meaningful in an extraordinary way receiving your hopes: when you disclose yourself to me, when you are yourself for me.

Here is an important question—for example, if I were admitted to a graduate school somewhere far away, would you come with me?

With my heart,
Adam

4/17/2009

My dearest Natalia, who reminds me that in sleep we do not part, while I needlessly insist on the formality of beginnings and endings, which for me are like stone markers in endlessly shifting sands.

In a way, I have been spoiled: your presence is the easiest and safest way to secure understanding;

in your presence I am safe in the sureness of our
thoughts, which move us and speak us, which run
their course.

That is nothing like the agony of arresting a
flow of thoughts and crafting them into static
presentation which must nevertheless tell you a
fluidity of feelings seen through a thoughtfulness
which is hard to explain.

That free interaction of our thoughts in our
presence is nothing like the agony of meditation:
what I write to you is indebted to thinking for a
long time. I fathom myself and wait: for those
things which need to be told to desultorily surface;
and the concentration is to keep it all arrayed
before me. My strength is garnered from the will
to a clear telling.

Well, I have to tell you something: today too
many things surfaced and they overflowed me.
I could not order them in that careful way. But
I want to give you evidence of the work I was
engaged in throughout the day. Today I have
failed to give you my thoughts. To make up for it,
I have tried to explain how I think for you.

I therefore await your presence. We will catch my
overflowing thoughts in a conversation containing
both of us, which will run its course: so that
we can do some of that work together which I
described.

For now, it is very important to me that you
receive the fullness of a wish that you enjoy
yourself tonight.

Adam

4/23/2009

Dear Natalia,

I fell out of the sky into a lake or from the lake
into the sky.

4/29/2009

Dear Natalia,

I wish you would call. I wish that you were
asleep. I am at your mom's house. My way here
was very peaceful. I rode the train and the 38.
There were not very many people on the bus, and
I felt relaxed as we rode up San Francisco toward
the shore. I looked at all of the people on the train
and tried to imagine what kind of lives they live.
I was wondering where in the world the rules for
the implications of what one looks like are kept.
That sentence can be interpreted many ways; I
mean for its significance to be an amalgamation
of those interpretations. I think that to be on the
outside requires two things—and the people on
the outside are on some kind of inside amongst
themselves—: (1) to understand consciously what
everyone else lives transparently, and (2) —and

this follows from (1)— to be free to bend the
rules; this is what makes an artist subversive; she
embarrasses everyone in her revealing: many acts
of creation are the learning process, the exposing
of the transparent.

When watching old people one should know they
were once young; when looking at young people,
that they will be old.

I began to write this before you called.

Adam

5/7/2009

Natalia,

I speak to you as myself, as that self which
remains responsible, alone, which has experienced
with you and by you—which in its best moments,
and in its worst moments, wants to destroy
the sacred autonomy between us, wants to
possess you; and in its best moments, and in its
worst moments, wants to set you free from all
expectations into the wideness that surrounds us.

Yes, this has been building up in the potentiality
of our minds for a long time, to be released in one
of those singular moments that, this time, in its
terror, defines history: casts the moments before
and after it into relief, providing a point from
which to see, to narrate, a point from which all
moments may gain their significance.

I am here. I am me.

I have seen what matters now, and that is to understand each other: to release you and us from the burden of having to maintain lies, illusions; to repair the rift between us so that we may see clearly.

5/15/2009

Dear Natalia,

If you were to see me walking down the street, you would give so much to me: you would save me from merely walking down the street. You would make my clothes speak. You would make my beard grow. You would misunderstand mere walking, and thus you would have me, and you would give to me. That is why.

Adam

5/18/2009

Did you know what I was talking about, when I talked about walking down the street?

There are many boring ways to explain what I meant. My beard grows because you have seen it grow. It is about the length of the present moment. Our history stretches the present moment into

the past and the future. I mean ours. You save me
from merely walking down the street. In other
words, you know me. But one can't just say that:
the vital moment needs to be revitalized somehow.
I mean this one or that one.

A question: Would it be good or bad to be content
completely in watching light through leaves? I
want everything. I'm not joking.

From the black, plastic seats at graduation, I
looked far above the podium to the light registered
in swirling motes among fresh, green leaves. I
left the commencement speech and leaned over to
you: "Isn't the light beautiful?" The reception was
inside a wooden building.

Adam

5/20/2009

I can't stand sending messages into nowhere. It
makes me feel like I am going crazy.

A spinning confusion.

Where are you?

I remain,
Adam

5/26/2009

Dear Natalia,

I don't understand.

I mean that I need to talk to you. Please use words to tell me.

It is hard for me not to know how you are. It is very hard for me not to know how you are. I still want to know when you sleep.

I come to you for reality. Please give it to me by speaking to me.

I see us walking through open fields, speaking.

Where are you? I just need to know you. Write to me. Will you ever write to me?

Truthfully, I remain,
Adam

7/8/2009

Dear Natalia,

I love you.

What are you doing? Why?

I want you to find me. Please find me.

Adam

Dear Natalia,

You remain so dear to me.

I called to ask, in a particular voice, "Would you like it if I wrote something for you?"

I have many words and thoughts for you, all of which work towards this: to explain myself to you, so that you will be freed, if you are not, to speak to me.

This is what I mean. Sometimes a great calm soothes me, and I smile at the simplicity of something that was underneath one's nose for a long time: "If we only could speak to one another! If only we were transparent like water, could see each other through and through, and were pacified by the good intentions thus disclosed! If only she would open herself to me, respond to my pleas, my sorrow at not being able to reach her. If only... I know that all would be well; for it could not be otherwise! If only we spoke honestly and openly, all would resolve."
I then smile at my anxiety and care, in knowing that such a solution, pure, naive and simple, lies so ready at hand. I think to myself that I need not even write to you: "I will allow my thoughts and feelings to flow from me at their will in her presence, thus enhancing their truthfulness from spontaneity; and come what may, I will have been honest; and she means so much to me, that I don't see how anything could go wrong." I prepare

myself for your feelings, your true feelings, needs, worries.

I try to call only for this; I cannot reach you.

My greatest fear is that you shall become a symbol to me of the impossibility of a certain closeness in human relations, in which I have faith; so that I will forever cherish the lock of your hair in solitude.

At this point, your destructive way of relating to me—I will say so—, our cooperative destruction, has now destroyed all expectations. This brings great sorrow, but also opportunity; and nothing has fallen to oblivion.

Do you understand? Something unspeakably important to my entire life depends on your understanding. I wish that you sometimes would ask me the same thing: "Do you understand?"

Natalia! I just want us to understand each other.

When we were apart, did you truly think of me so often? You were a silent seed in me whose growth could not be repressed: your seed bloomed into an unstoppable life inside me, whose thirst fixated lovingly upon you. It shot through me suddenly, and I now live and will always. It was as if you were sleeping inside me, and then your independence, your will, your fullness overcame and animated me, and left me changed.

Where are you?

I remain,
your,
Adam

Dear Natalia,

I tell myself you must be ignorant of the suffering
you cause.

I woke this morning thinking that it was some sort
of accident that I should be able to slip these notes
under a door that is closed to me. I asked myself,
"Where would I be if it weren't possible for me to
slip these notes under her door?"

I implore you with all my heart to speak to me—
at least, to have courtesy.

I had a thought yesterday, that maybe I am a
mystery to you, even though I try so hard to show
myself to you. You know me well enough to have
uncovered the contradictions, the questions, the
confused mixture of elements inside me. If you
are alarmed just ask me about them. I will not
keep anything from you. Just ask me.

I worry that you have set a trap for yourself, and
if so all I want to do is help you out of it: that in
keeping yourself in a way hidden from me, you
believe that all people do this, so that you have
trouble trusting me, because you think that I do
the same.

You leave me to myself to understand you, in a
terrible loneliness, in which I constantly wish that
your own presence would help me understand
you.

In despair I whisper to myself, "If we could only
speak..."

Please be fair to me. Please. This is all I can say.
This is all I can do.

Adam

7/20/2009

Dear Natalia,

Please write to me.

Adam

7/21/2009

My dear Natalia,

I know that it can be hard to understand the
mixture of this consciousness and self-control
with what you rightly called a 'frenzy.'

When I gain perspective—when I see clearly—,
I look at my behavior and think that I am foolish;
then I feel that I am a hypocrite—and I know a

69

hypocrite is something you cannot stand. But to
be quite self-conscious of one's own growth—
to have a clear record of one's past and one's
present—puts one at greater risk of not knowing
how to understand the incongruousness of one's
former self with one's present self.

But I know that somehow my frenzied resistance
served a purpose. The resistance helped us to
understand each other: even if that cannot be
explained, I believe you know that it is true. It
helped me break through you, which revealed just
a little of what is inside, but which you had to
hide on principle, which I had to know in order to
understand.

This is what is important: I have now experienced
the understanding that you needed to show me
something which you could not show me in any
other way

I say this not free from worry; I say what I believe
but also what I want to believe.

Love,
Adam

Sometimes I lose perspective to the beauty of a
singular vision. At other times I lose my single
vision to the multitude of perspectives to which
I have access. This pitiful and tragic loss I used
to experience too often in the past. Fear of this is
what has led me to call devotion beautiful. But as
with all things: balance.

Dear Natalia,

I woke up this morning at 3:30 from a long sleep.
I forgot to turn my alarm off, set yesterday; for a
moment I thought I was leaving you.

In the dark I tried to remember whether I'd eaten
dinner, whether I'd brushed my teeth.

Then a feeling so overwhelming that it makes me
cower came over me. It is so unspeakable, and it
makes everything that is mine new to me, so that
in this uncanny new light I feel the oddness of my
own destiny. The feeling can be so intense that it
almost makes me nauseous, but this feeling is so
arresting, that in its moment all the other available
absurdities of life fall away from me, leaving me
free in my complete but accidental concentration
on what it means to be. Then I contrast this
feeling with the billions of lives I know to exist,
which in this time cannot but appear to me as the
blind life force.

Then there is nothing that makes me question
what I am doing, nor why I am doing it: thoughts
about all the people sleeping in their beds, the
tremendous portion of history that I have not read,
the words and languages that I do not know—all
my questions do not bother me, they find repose
within me.

And I want to say to you what I know. I love you.

This amidst my youth and uncertainty, fear that I will change, that we will grow apart.

Now after I have written to you, the intensity of the feeling is gone: its force that obliterates all need for pacing and justification wanes.

I look at you plaintively and questioningly, as I look at myself.

Your,
Adam

8/1/2009

Dear Natalia,

When you show nothing of yourself, I have nothing but myself to get lost in—and I do get lost if you will not make an effort to correct me.

Teach me to be able to understand without words; help me in this, as I will help you with your words.

Recalling how we have been, all the moments in which we have known each other, with or without words, in the past few weeks, I am overwhelmed by the way conflict between us seems inevitably to lift us both; as if, when we strike each other, even out of anger and fear, neither of us weakens, but after each strike, we strengthen, return a

stronger blow, and thus honor and lift each other
in contest.

But please understand that I want to be weak for
you: I want to be so weak for you, showing you I
understand that the contest is for good; that we put
on a hardened face because we must in the name
of our individuality—but that we love to be weak,
so weak and tender for each other.

When you asked me, "Do you want to seem
needy?" it was as if you were talking about
yourself.

Adam

8/3/2009

Dear Natalia,

I am safely in Europe.

My uncle's apartment overlooks a River in
Catalonia. The faces of the apartments are painted
yellow, blue, red.

We are nine hours ahead here.

I saw the sun rise twice.
Awake, I imagined your warmth and the
sleepiness of your breath in the morning.

Tell me something,
Adam

8/6/2009

Dear one,

I called tonight, but your cell phone wouldn't
work.

Now I am downstairs in a public internet room in
a hotel in Paris.
If I could write to you freely, and if I were capable
of telling you what I want you to know I feel—
and right now I am not capable, I just can't—then
I would enervate myself by writing to you. I
would rather use all my energies writing to you
now then use them to see Paris tomorrow, but only
if I were capable of telling you how I feel right
now; and I am incapable—and I am here, and it
is silly not to be here. Yes, I would gladly flop
around on the floor in true exhaustion, but only
with a guarantee that my writing will give you
the feelings I felt tonight walking on the streets;
which is a preposterous condition given that one
has got life all wrong, sadly and pitifully wrong, if
one is looking for guarantees.

Love,
Adam

8/11/2009

Dear Natalia,

I feel so powerless. I would like to tear up all the
pages I have ever written to you, in frustration,
then beg your forgiveness for tearing them up; and
then I would really hope with all my heart that
you would try to put them all back together again.
Can you see me with little pieces of shredded
paper all over the place, like snow?

If I spent all my life trying to say something, and
I wrote down some notes, and I was sitting on a
bench, then if the wind blew the paper out of my
hands, right now I would be too tired to chase it
down the street; instead, I would just touch your
hands.

Adam

8/16/2009

My dear, dear, dear Natalia, sweetest Natalia,

Your mom insisted that I stay in Paris longer—
and so I am: I was going to leave last Friday, now
I will stay until Tuesday night.

Walking around in the gardens at Versailles, I was
calmed in that vast, ordered domain dedicated
to health and living. The geometrical forms
protected me from the nonsensical entropy of the
universe, and I felt at ease within this expansive
but limited horizon: looking far off to where the
immense rectangular pools end, lined with trees,
and the human forms carved in marble, cherubs
riding sphinxes, their plump, sensual bodies and

the well-defined muscles of a warrior; the feet of a
woman walking in a garden.

I thought about living only for health: a peaceful,
clearheaded ruthlessness, which would make all
hardship, every difficult human relationship fall
away from me passively, as I dedicate myself
to these buoyant forms, this paradise of gilded
ceilings and lightsome mirrors.

I then thought this was a terrible daydream.

This morning I wish for home. I love to fret over
your little womb, your warmth, your delight. It
is so good to care about things that hold us to the
earth.

We may be confused.

Love,
Adam

8/17/2009

Dear Natalia,

I thought about the thread that connects us: I
thought that I do not know your thoughts, where
you are. Here it is night and there it is day. I
experience a passionate joy and sadness here.
Often I wish for you to point things out to me: the
pattern of the worn wood on a palace floor, the
fineness of some fabric, the way in which a little
girl pushes a miniature sailboat with a stick in

a fountain, preposterousness of so many people
and things here. I search inside myself for your
impulsiveness as I walk through the markets: I
buy grapes, peaches, bread for later. I try to build
inside myself as I see, the counterpart to my sight:
words that will help me show you and tell you
things I have thought and seen. I carry it within
me, a towering list, until it tumbles over me: and I
am lost in the immediacy of my own experience,
a painful joy. So many daydreams: they are
beautiful, they fill me with a naive longing: and
sometimes dread when I am lost and do not
know whether they are silly and impossible,
whether they would please you; when I think they
wouldn't I blush so painfully inside: I tug at my
hair. I feel that I am neither here nor there. I want
to reach out for all the beautiful people that I see,
but my sight overflows my words: and I don't
have anything to say except: you are here, but my
arms are not wide enough to embrace you.

I send you my tiny, little embrace, and I hope to
warm you with it and to fill myself with you.

Adam

8/21/2009

Dear Natalia,

Elope with me.

Every time I have blown an eyelash from your
fingertips, I have wished that you will marry me.

I have worried that our minds are like open windows battering against the house in the wind, loose on their hinges. I withdraw in fear when I worry that we don't understand each other. You say to me plainly, when I worry about madness, that it is not necessary. And you point out to me that I am me and you are you, and we aren't anybody else, so that we can't worry about what will happen!

The frantic ant, the black dot scurrying on the face of the burning flagstone, which you conjured for me in one of your moods, for you and me senselessness and absurdity, when I know what is what, at certain times when I think of you, it does not worry me.

All the many and various paths of life, crisscrossing themselves through space and time in senseless confusion—at times like these I think: What does that concern me? I am myself.

And all this, even though I know that when seen externally, my sayings and my convictions can't but seem like some sort of personal insanity. I persist through this. I can point out one thousand more contradictions and confusions within myself; and at the same time I insist that this is no excuse—and I don't know for what I would use it as an excuse, anyway!

I have many things to tell you. Thank God that your ears hear. When you next speak with me, say

to me, Adam, you said you have many things to
tell me. And I will begin to tell you.

I mean everything I have ever said to you, else I
am nothing more than swirling air with no ground
of my own.

There are many, many words to be spoken, soon.

Trust,
Adam

8/21/2009

Dear Natalia,

I just had an idea, though it certainly isn't mine
because I've come across it before, but it just
struck me:
Most people are kept in life, in the flow of life,
and therefore fulfilled, even when they don't
know it, by external necessities.

Art has to be made by an inner necessity, to make
up for that break that must be made in the flow
of life for creation, because otherwise the break
makes a hole that can't be filled: for a break with
flow of impulse and necessity must be made in
order to create the space of freedom in which art
is done. The wholesomeness of outer necessity
is that the question "Why?" is never asked: the
certain unowned dignity of a person to whom
it doesn't make any sense to ask why. This
wholesomeness must be given to inner necessity.

Why am I telling you this?

Adam

9/2/2009

Forgive me.

I can come over this evening.

Call me today.

9/27/2009

Dear Natalia,

"Never stop writing to me."

I suspend the following question in the air, a
floating question: What if to write I must awaken
a threatening spirit? I describe it vaguely, because
I believe that neither of us can put our finger on it.

Should I let go of the primordial desire that your
eyes should see what mine see?

Adam

9/28/2009

Dear Natalia,

Sometimes I feel embarrassed; and yesterday, I felt humiliation.

I feel humiliated when I believe you have been secretly watching my true movements from some hiding place.

I feel humiliated when you don't take responsibility for yourself, leaving me alone.

I feel sometimes the dread of something falling away from me, not being able to figure out why, like when I visited you that one time, such a long time ago: you were capable of acting as if we had never shared ourselves with each other. It was as if I were trapped inside myself: you had stolen my voice from me, by denying that it had ever spoken to you—not merely denying, but by neither denying nor affirming: as if it didn't exist, as if I had made it up by myself, alone.

In front of the world, you make me seem crazy—

Sincerely,
Adam

9/29/2009

I am struck now by the memory of the way your hair felt on my face when I nuzzled into it at the park a long time ago.

10/3/2009

Dear Natalia,

In a closed box on my shelf I have a lock of your
hair, unseen everyday, but there, as you are in my
mind. My faith is, letting go.

I am pushed by life, and I wish there were no
hurry. I remember how my life felt safe when we
talked about growing old, and when you pointed
out old men who were dignified, and reassured me
that I can be like that.

I am at "at a loss".

I wish you would call me back when I call you.

Sometimes I don't think you need to say anything.
But then I feel like I am blind and confused, and
that you are not honest.

I'll always be,
Adam

10/5/2009

I'm like a sailboat, floating around in a sheltered
cove—but the weather is nice; sky rather
perspicuous.

See me floating around, out past the breakers at
Stinson Beach, lying in corpse pose on the deck

of my boat, on a brisk, autumnal day; water like
sunlight on quicksilver.

Sharks flounder around below. One forgives them
for their sublimity, because they are sharks being
sharks.

Adam

10/6/2009

Natalia,

I don't know whether the world laughs behind my
back. Is it laughable to wonder what the world
laughs about?

I will soon heave a gigantic sigh, exhaling my
whole life; then I will breathe it back in again.

I say all these things to you without urgency—
without a certain kind of naive urgency. I don't
even mean them to be momentous: then I would
have to commit myself completely to their
reception within you—and now I do not know
you and myself well enough.

I feel so despicable. If I write to you more, the
feeling will only increase. I put your hair on my
mantel, but then I put it way in a drawer.
It felt absurd. It felt like I was denigrating myself.
Speaking to you kindly does violence to me,
somehow. Yet, when I do not think, it is only
natural to be kind.

83

And all is well. I do not know what I want—

I wanted to take a quiet bath with you tonight,
to help you rub salts and oils into your calves, to
fondle your feet, and to run my hands through the
hair below your stomach. I wanted to talk about
life and what you thought about it.

Sometimes I think you would like me to be free—
but I just am free, don't you get it?

Walking about, especially at night, and especially
below an open sky, I feel peaceful and clearheaded. I then wish to transmit this lucidness to
you.

I am thinking of writing our memories for
you. The only way that I could get past my
own degenerate state so that this task became
conceivable was to tell you that I am writing them
to you so that you can read them when you are
old. Before that, I thought that I would write our
memories for you so that I would stir your insides
a little bit so that your voice wouldn't speak to me
indifferently on the telephone. That seemed like
a bad reason. Of course, I would also write them
for myself. I would even aspire to write them so
that they would be worthwhile to someone wholly
other than us; but one shouldn't set out thinking
like that, because it is so conceited, and silly in
front of the night sky—it may be used as a very
vague atmospherical inspiration, but not as a
principal motivator.

I am going to give myself up to possibility. You
will find me very, very quiet. I will smile at you
while you speak to me, but I won't respond unless
you say something extraordinary.

I am going to give myself up to possibility,
knowing that, anyway, you still breathe, as do I.

So I mean this: I am alright. I don't believe I am
presumptuous when I tell you that

I am alright,
Adam

10/7/2009

Dear Natalia,

I never wanted thought to be difficult; it should
be like walking easily. I never mean to trap you:
I just go where I go, and I try to say clearly and
easily what is what; and conclusions that follow
from premises don't always mean very much,
anyway.

Again, forgive me, for I do not know how I find
you. Do you understand what I mean?

People are prone to facile characterizations; with
that said, I recognize that I am imbalanced. I'll
leave it at that and trust that you know me well
enough to know what I mean. I will set off my
next claim with a dash—-but so are you.

You rush ahead without thought, I fall behind with thought.

I don't know why you resist me so much.

Do you have a presentiment of a weighty darkness in me? This is just my way, another way, of getting at that which is your favorite excuse: whimsy, capricious mystery; which is not a good excuse.

The mystic is foremost a master of the practical; versed in body and spirit—perhaps more in touch with the body than someone "very spiritual"—he knows the order of exigencies: practical stability first, allowing one to be the master of one's own domain, so that one can be unstable at will, not destabilized.

I don't know if I can overcome my didacticism by pointing out how flimsy everything I am saying is. (This is a token of what seems to be a blight in my mind.)

Take what is useful, leave the rest behind; but be responsible to people—what would the world be without them?

Society is like the organic complexity of the interrelations of beings in an ecosystem. What a silly and obvious statement. I meant to point out that it should be as difficult to understand people as it is to understand ecosystems: sometimes the secret importance of a being in an ecosystem is

veiled; sometimes something that looks like a
waste of space is vitally important.
If one knows this connectedness, one's opinions
of other people are tempered. I am defending a
personal inconsistency: you sometimes think that
I look down my nose at everyone while claiming
that I don't. These points have something to do
with resolving that.

Adam

10/7/2009

Dear Natalia,

Last night, before I fell asleep, I imagined writing
something to you that would say once and for
all just exactly how I feel.

I think it is worthwhile for me to explain to you
my fits of anxiety. These begin, these fits of
anxiety, as a result of exposing myself to you, in
written words, without being able to know how
you receive me. It is like being watched through
a one-way mirror by the person whom you wish
to reach; being confined to see nothing but the
protracted movements of your own reflection, as
they become disconnected and absurd, deprived
of the only thing in reference to which they make
sense—you. I don't expect you to understand
this, because you have never tried it. When I
call you twenty times, it is after looking into this
terrible mirror for too long, and it is only natural
that I should have absolutely nothing to say: I am

87

seeking to see past the mirror, to make myself
whole again.

Do you remember how you wept as I combed
your hair?

Goodbye Natalia,
Adam

I will always be your friend. I am not saying this
to angrily punctuate the difficult things I have
said.

10/12/2009

Dear Natalia,

Thank you for talking to me.

I believe what I said: that we can find meaning
by understanding that we help each other grow.
(Without this, I am lost).
Forgive me when growth makes me hypocritical.
At times I made you feel that in some way I
couldn't live in the world without you. Forgive
me for this selfishness.

Please forgive me.
I think about life, and as you said, it is easy to get
caught in normal ways of "thinking about life"
so that one stops really seeing it, the suffering in
the world; when I think about life, and I really
see it, everything seems so inexplicable that I get

lost. I believe paradoxically that we are and aren't
responsible for our lives. It is impossible.
This is not an excuse.
To write this to you, it is as if something
important is falling out of my hands, like sand
slipping through my fingers.
I don't know what it is.
I know that you love me.
I wonder how you even understand me after
everything I've written to you.
You used to tell me sometimes after I wrote things
to you and I was worried, "No, it isn't crazy at
all."
It always meant very much to me when you said
that.

Your,
Adam

11/3/2009

It comes out of me to say: the world is wrong
that I cannot see you. That I cannot see you and
everything that you do. I mean everything: what
you do to be away from me, even. The world
seems wrong that I cannot know not being able
to see you; that you shouldn't be lost to me in the
presence of your absence in a place that I long for
and long to call here, where we are, where I can
see you and not seeing you.

I feel so bad. I am struck again by words and the
way I can tell you things. I am trapped in my

room: I am trapped in a room that is supposed to be shelter, because I cannot see far enough.

I feel so bad.

11/5/2009

You're a human being.

12/5/2009

The blank notebook is all you have left for you.

It is not right that you should keep me at arms length because I know you.
The feelings I have for you are so deep that they threaten my practical mind.

I have been childish and dependent. But it would be a wrongdoing to understand me without understanding what I look for. You have told me I am selfish. This is another lesson I have learned, but which I can't be sure I learned from you.

You taught me to love the colors of the leaves on trees.

This is your lesson, whether or not you have tried to teach it: that I press too hard against life, that I do not let it rest, that I do not let it come into its own

12/10/09

Dear Natalia,

Just to offer a little more insight into how I'm doing, for me or for you, I don't know anymore.

I feel sick. I'm tired of constantly feeling like I see farther than most people: I censure myself for this feeling. I try to make it none of my concern what I know in comparison to what other people know. I try not to ever think like that because it is ugly and immoral to me. Yet I am overcome with doubts and feelings like this.

I would do whatever possible to show that I understand that my case is in no way extraordinary, that I am in no way asking for special consideration from anybody.

All this and I still want to go about and live, and then I feel a banal disappointment: I mean an ordinary feeling without extraordinary origins that comes about when I look at the average run of things, even if I will myself to follow the maxim "If you don't have anything good to say, don't say anything at all."

For most people consciousness gains coherency because they are what they are fixed into a nexus of social relations. It's like they are a node bound in place, defined, and activated by the strength of these connections between people. They can't become intellectually terrorized by 8 billion people in the world because their position in the nexus filters everything and fashions everything in their own image: nothing is seen that doesn't pertain to them in some coherent way—to what end, it doesn't matter. I got dislodged from the nexus, so I'm not even my mother's son. Nothing seems coherent, just crazy or beyond my grasp. Beyond my grasp is indeed a safer way to understand things. To live with mental coherence I have had to make 'that which is beyond my grasp' a God in front of whom I humble myself and recognize as my superior. I actually pray, but it is just a mantra that calms me: "Dear me or God or the world, my life is small, subject to forces beyond my control, be they blind or sighted." It is more than something I just say; I don't know why I should be reluctant to admit it.

I don't really rely on or care about most of what I just said: they are nice words, but I don't invest much in this 'social nexus' theory as it relates to 'consciousness." I mean that to make up things like that is silliness: hubris if not understood in the right way.

I don't know any other way to live than to be honest and fair, temperately human, good to those that I love, and kind to everyone I meet, saving my own opinions for people and things that truly matter, without passing any sort of judgment on the world regarding 'what matters.'

I will not let anyone steal my warmth from me, what I am, and what I can give. I will make my own love if I have to. Silly proclamations.

I feel well,
X

12/14/2009

It is clear to me that I have been stringing together
platitudes for most of my life; that for fear of the
banality and sincere difficulty of the practical
world I have inflated my experiences with
highfalutin words; that I have tried to forgive you
by imagining you as I must; that I have acted like
a child with an incurable darkness and suspicion;
that I have been essentially intolerant; that I have
withheld myself from people for fear of failure;
that I have hoped in an endlessly embarrassing
and humiliating way for the extraordinary; that
I have conflated mania and genius; that for all
my efforts the simplest aspects of my self remain
frighteningly, ridiculously, and humanly opaque;
that I want to live.

6/14/2010

Reading what I have written, thinking about what
you have said to me over time, what I have felt,
what we have done, I discover so much confusion
and pain that I wonder if one can ever get it right:
say something simply and clearly, so it rings true
and stays. It seems that life is something one gets
lost in. I'm always trying to get hold of this thing
that gets away, which causes grief and confusion.
Memories begin to seem useless when
thoughts recorded on paper begin to show their

shortcomings: they seem a mass of changing
feelings that highlight the disintegration of
convictions.
As time passes, I don't know what to do or say,
and all the artifacts of my life seem useless,
adventitious—words that I have written and
spoken.
And yet, I am certain that I love you: I need to be
certain that I love you, as I love the world and my
own life.

My devotion to you was to be something that
flew high above all of this, something constant,
indestructible, clear and true. It was so much folly.

I don't know where I have gotten myself, perhaps
the knowledge that there is virtue in simplicity
and going with the flow. When I see the things
of this world in their fading brightness, when I
see them integrated and meaningful within the
entire context of humanity, situated within and
connected by so many lives, so many countless
lives, I am decided that I am better for everything:
I am better that my childish naïveté and juvenile
philosophical conceits have been tempered by
worldly disappointment and suffering. It was only
a token of this childishness, when in your bed,
wearing your white nightgown, you asked me to
promise to always help you grow—when I am
the one who must learn! I foolishly believed so
strongly in myself and myself alone that I became
blind to the world, destroyed fragile joy and my
natural inclination to experience joy with other
people.

Whether or not I reach you—this, in any case,
is no longer my selfish desire: that only I reach
someone, that only I be understood—, whether or
not you believe or understand this, I tell myself
that through you I have learned to live again, that
I have recovered something forgotten.

I am sorry for being needlessly complicated, in
the past and now. Call me whenever you want and
we can talk about our lives in an easier way. I can
tell you about my garden.
I would gladly be your friend, outside of previous
expectations, outside of past and deeply human
desires.
I would like to be fresh and open to you,
as fresh and open as I can be, but without
hurtfully wanting to forget, or to deny, that I
have loved you, that I know you.

Out of seemingly endless confusion, but also from
easy joy, clarity, and forgetfulness; despite my
black worries that hope in understanding is lost—
This is the best that I can do. It really is.

I don't want to write so many romantic and
highfalutin sentences anymore. If you want to, I
wish that we can talk more easily and naturally in
the future.

Adam

Do you remember when we cycled to the beach,
two persons on one bike?
Do you remember when you spit water on my
face from the drinking fountain by the tennis
courts?

I don't need to be so grave. Just be my friend, it
means the world to me.
There is nothing to lose, only meaning to be
gained.

I struggle to be happy because I hear so many
horrible things all of the time; I feel the sanest and
most at peace in Nature.
I did something stupid: I put my first garden
somewhat in the shade of a tree.

When I was much younger, many years ago, I
imagined my dream house: when visiting me, one
had to leave all instruments of time at the door,
outside. There were no clocks in this house. If
absolutely necessary an invisible alarm could be
set for visitors, so the world could beckon them
back. It is interesting that this is what I imagined:
not the building, not where it was, but the absence
of time.

I always hope that you are well, wherever you are,
whatever you are doing.

Epilogue

Do you remember when I told you I wished I could write down what happened? I was desperate. We were at a restaurant by the sea. In the stillness of time, I despaired of capturing your uniqueness which exceeds all measure: this ground I can never stand on. I needed the security of what had happened, even if I'd already died in the blaze. I see now that I was desperate for you to exist: otherwise I'd die. So for the sake of being, I withstood your scorn and became its possibility. You delighted in my desire for eternity, spurring me on toward you. You needed to exist, just as I do, and mercilessly assured me I would be able to do it: write it down. My darling, little dove, I know that we were accomplices in obscure love, in whose brokenness I have become what I am. You are my heart, at the center of everything and beyond it. I have become capable of loving you, just as you are.

I feel nothing but benevolent wonder when I witness myself groveling at your feet. I cried and cried, pleading with you to forgive me. That my sobbing and explaining should have only intensified your cruelty created an opening. Can you imagine what it would be like to burn alive? In that emanation of light, it is very quiet. In desperation, I literally kissed your feet. It was better to remain guilty, preserving the possibility of explanation, than to be merely harrowed by the naked world. Unbelievably, I'd done nothing wrong, yet together we made it possible for an innocent person to plead forgiveness. At such extremes, two sides of the same made way for a miracle. One day, I woke up and gently broke the chains of human reason. It is inexplicable, hence the miraculousness. Innocence and guilt, undone at their origin. Sometimes there is the old will toward redemption, yet what I noticed after this burning is that there is nothing to transfigure. This is what I mean by my capability: I love you as you are.

I have kept artifacts, but they are nothing but that which knows them. In one photograph, a jagged edge of light gives the appearance that I will be engulfed in the flames of an approaching fire. Like anything else, it is impossible to trace these words to their origin. And that I should think of burning. These words appear, as you did one day, sitting on a bench at the edge of campus. It's not even that you appeared there, but that you are still here somehow. Can I trust in the appearance of these words? They appear, anyway, and I am learning what freedom means.

During the course of our shared existence, you told me to write to you always. It was a provocative conceit that appealed well to my passionate origin. What does *always* mean? It is a mystery to me.

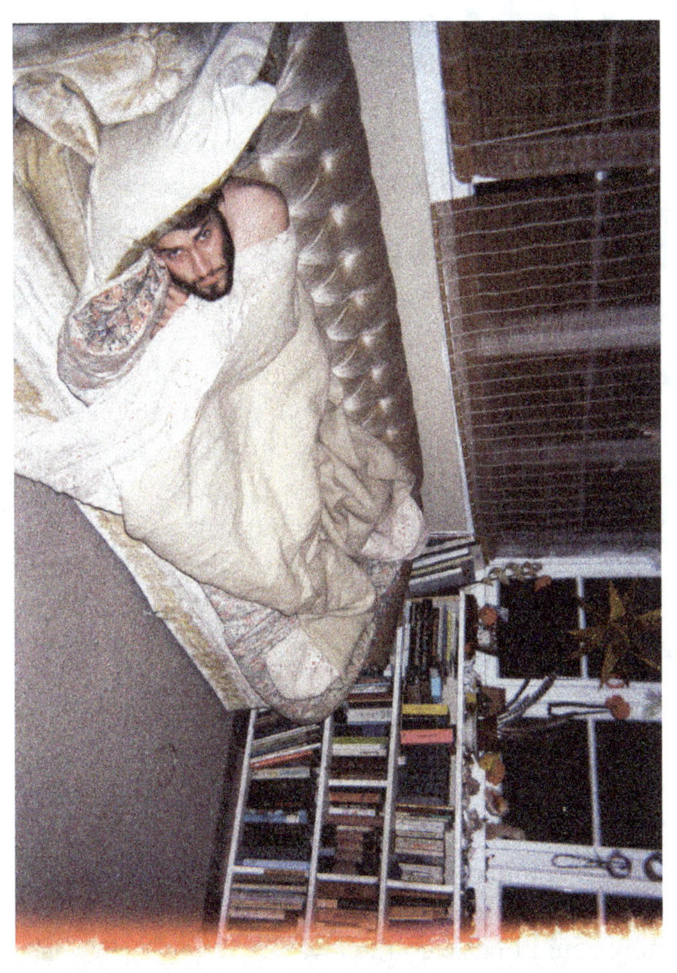

Always write to me, you demanded. I am awestruck. There is stillness now, when I remember: an encompassing stillness filled with unceasing movement. I whisper your words in astonishment—always write to me—and wonder about them. It is incredible that you demanded this, that you could even think it. You furiously exacted the absolute from my relative existence. From my crestfallen, desperate brilliance. What does it even mean? You are absolutely brutal, throwing me back on myself and enjoying my humiliation. I am brutalized. I felt your brutality, and it was your tenderness that made me bow my head. I felt your heart's tenderness while burning alive.

What kind of demand was that to make of a human being? I knew your brutality like the softest torment teasing me into life, and I am liberated through bewilderment: that being itself allows us to entertain the impossible. I just had to be the certainty of this promise to you. As if to prove that we exist. It was my will, to prove that we exist. I bound myself to you, dear heart, to show us that we exist. I bound myself, and I was lost to willfulness. As if it had been necessary, to bind myself. But how could I have gotten away?

It's funny now, while I'm crying. You teach me the tearful laughter of certain death. Through itself, the willfulness has been undone, as I return to everything. I hear your word *always*—this hope that we are miraculously allowed to have and which you inhumanly demanded of me—and everything is quiet, like a candle flame in darkness.

Apparently you wanted me to experience something. How else can it be explained?

My love, we do not want the infinite. We are in love with the finite and wish that it would never end. This is what I know, after disentangling myself from your annihilating longing. I am separate now, and free to die. Feeling in myself alone that ungodly, breathtaking vitality in being the speck of dust you imagined me to be. You looked at me, with a promise in your eyes, only to single me out and belittle me. Everything I needed, you spit on, while pretending to console me. You showed me that I was a worthless speck of dust, and I was only too willing to collude in your murderous fantasy: that we are timeless and one. But this is only half true, my love. We are not two, but we are not one. And we'll just have to live with that.

My God, I have never been so humiliated, throwing myself at your feet. I needed you, and you belittled my wholeness, only because it has an end. I needed you, because I am whole. I needed you, and you disfigured my wholeness, only because it has an end. You hated my neediness, which I have only because I am whole. I just needed you. In my ignorance, I had to protect myself from you, colluding in your murderous fantasy: that we are timeless and one. While promising to console me, you used this to undermine me. You opened the cosmos, only to compare me. I know your love in your lies. I know your lies as an expression of love. Your hopeful lies, in which the world is reflected, and I no longer need protection. You lying whore! I am beyond compare.

For what was I being prepared? In you, I saw an end to my suffering. In our broken love that longed to transcend: I saw you, an end to my suffering. Has anyone ever been so used? I was sorry, until I was changed. There is no way out. Besides, you used me, too. It was the same, but different. You also needed to go beyond. The pain we never talked about compelled you to go beyond. In a frenzy, you went beyond yourself, using me. Your seduction was my terror. I was terrorized when you told me to consume you. And I wanted to exist with you beyond, but I could not find you there. I could never find you there, and it was terrifying. I was enthralled by your suicidal superiority, and you exploited me utterly.

You would point, in your bouts of madness, to something beyond words. You were larger than life, in your holiness which battened on my mortality. You spurned me in your superiority, pointing beyond yourself. I wanted to be superior, too, because I wanted to meet you. But I could not find you there. It was terrifying to be so alone. And when I did glimpse you, a mess of childlike tears, you sanctimoniously pointed beyond, calling on saints to make your case. Sometimes, I glimpsed you. You asked me to brush your sandy-blonde hair. I was undone by your tenderness. When I touched you, your overwhelming need shattered me. And then, again, you were wanton and holy, telling me we would always be one, beyond everything. What were you trying to do? You are not holy. You are human. Must I apologize, after all this, for not being a saint? I am not. I never was: only in your eyes. There is nothing to be sorry about. There is no way out.

In spite of your distance, I found you, my love. You wanted to be beyond reach, because you were so afraid. You were so terrified that you became holy, spurning me. Your numinous sex that devastated me, and the blissfulness that tore through my world. I worshipped you and wanted to return to nothing, but you wouldn't let me. I was not good enough for you as I am.

As if you were beyond words! What sanctimoniousness. You hypocrite, with your distance and longing to be consumed. These are my words for you! Who else's could they be? What sanctimoniousness! As if you were above life.

I used to wordlessly suffer. In a human world, I suffered wordlessness. Do you understand what that means? You demanded that I write to you always, and pointed beyond words. It is hilarious. You touched my innermost, dissolving me in pleasure and light. Filling me with emptiness. And then you showed me utter cruelty. You enjoyed barring me from you and watching what happened. What were you doing? You just watched. I burned alive, and you just watched. You just watched, confirming your distance, and that taught me everything. As if you were above life, and everyone is so ready to believe you. Everyone wants to believe you. But there is nothing to fear. I am with you now and I am rewarded: with my life.

I know the word as the possibility of silence. I know you as the possibility of beyond. I have become both and neither. I only wanted you, my dear heart. I only wanted you because you were apart from me. Now you are not, and I don't know who I am.

You insisted on my death and told me to write to you always. You told me to write to you always, while insisting that nothing would last. You told me that nothing would last, yet said that I should write always. You wanted me to make things forever, and told me this could not be.

You said we'll always be connected. Always, with a cosmic thread of gossamer. It was cruel when you put the cosmos between us. Weren't we one? And you said it to anyone who fell in love with only what he saw. I wanted you to say it to me. But who am I? I am anyone speaking everyone's language. I am who I am. It doesn't make any sense, my love. But what can I tell you?

* * *

In retrospect, it's astounding that you accused me of harming you. It is the brutal seed of miracle: that you accused me of harming you. I was terrorized when you told me to consume you, and felt I was being destroyed.

I was terrorized when you told me to consume you. And after I'd done your bidding, you annihilated me with shame. Wielding your accusations: triumphant arbiter, glinting like steel above the suffering tides. I was so scared of you. And I just wanted you to love me.

Am I the tenderness of life mirrored in its devastation? The absolute terror I felt when you drove me out of our home. I had no home without you. Why did you need to do that to me?

I sought your lightness against my gravity. Must we always take things so seriously? You asked me, must we always take things seriously? You made me laugh, teasing me, and I continued to exist so that you could devastate my love incarnate. In allowing you to lay waste to my being, I was competing in holiness. Look, there is nothing here to destroy. Here I am: beyond you.

We laughed together so often. It was maddeningly hilarious, when I almost had to restrain you. You were going to hurt yourself. It is hilarious, and I am choking on my tears while laughing that anyone believes you can be restrained.

You have torn me apart in contradiction. Loving and hating in equal measure tore me apart. I could only find myself beyond. When I am beyond, I don't know where I am. I don't know who I am.

I could not be burned alive by the one I love for no reason. I could not be burned alive by you, the one I love, for no reason.

It was so easy to take the blame. Whereas I had been set up. It was a set-up, whose purpose lies beyond me. I am changed, for reasons beyond me.

Nothing could convince me of my innocence: the innocence of the flames. The innocence of dying. The innocence of love. The innocence was too much to bear.

I might have touched you then, but you kept yourself aloof, wielding those impossible words that pinned me down. I just wanted to touch you, and you went beyond. Wielding the otherworldly judgment, so far away from here. It is the strangest love, and we are accomplices. I'm sorry that I lost sight of your brilliance by making you my judge. There's tenderness in those words, as if the past were released, until it becomes the easy-going intensity of the life beyond what I believed myself to be.

* * *

Why do I feel so denuded? I am so poor and alone, in an expanse. It is an overwhelming presence beyond me, but only I know it. I am afraid, but I do not know why. I remember how hard I fought with your ease. I believed you had a secret that was kept from me. I hated you for the secret of your freedom: you meant that much to me. For your obliviousness, I envied you. I hated oblivion with all my might and envied you for it. You were like a force of nature, and I felt trapped in human form. I envied your ability to destroy without thinking. I loved you, and you were just being yourself. I wanted to know how I could be that way. I just wanted to be free, like you. But I could not be free without knowing both sides. Searching for you has destroyed the world I live in.

It is like existing truly, this chaos for which I envied you, out of which my heart is born. I am speechless now in the face of your violence, which compels me to speak. But if you were to take me now, I would not be curtailed. There is nothing before me that you could take away. I live where there is nothing before me: and it is the only way I move on. I am joyful when you see through my eyes, but I do not know what you see.

I am still writing, and I do not know to whom. There is nobody here, yet I am writing. When I was a child, I thought I was writing to myself. Yet there must be someone: words prove this. So I am alone and never alone. Disconsolate, until seeing you. I am writing, but I don't know who you are. Once you had sandy-blonde hair and wore a blue skirt: like an upside-down flower. And I address you now. How do I see you? How do I know you? Are you me? I can't see you, but I know you. So, I have become blind while seeing. I am blind-sight. I am blind: now I see. It's a miracle.

You are everything to me, and I don't know who you are. Back then, it was so clear, but I couldn't find you. Everything was occluded, in my longing for you. Now I don't know who you are, and it is easier. My blindness gives me sight. I am devastated, but I can see. I am not the first, nor will I be the last. How did I go blind? How do I see? The grace of your violence took me beyond what is personal and impersonal. They are two sides of the same, and I am free in necessity. It does not make any sense, my love. But what can I tell you?

* * *

It is not a question whether I am guided. My life unfolds, does it not? You have shown me this. Somehow it happened.

I have become the mystery of tears. There is such stillness and ease, not like this theater of doubt in which I have suffered. Who could mistake you, who could blame you for your cruelty, while shedding such tears? They are miraculous and make me know peace. It's all the same. I can't rebel and I don't need to convince myself. It is just like the words: they come. I am not making any of this up. Who decides what happens? I am dying.

Your unpredictability being absolute: it only frightens me when we are apart. When we are together, as one, I don't know what I am doing, yet I am reassured. I am sheltered, and I don't know who is moving my hand. What am I capable of? It is so strange, the safety of your chaos. Sometimes, the difference confuses me. How am I to live at peace with you, my heart? How? With all that I love. And my certain death. I know that you love me, because you hate me. Am I confused? There is no difference. I am not trying to be clever! You used to tease me about my seriousness. Sometimes it is unbearable. Still I dare to know you. Dying with my eyes open in the searing flames. How strange to find shelter in your chaos.

As you initiated me into the mystery of suffering, I gradually noticed the obvious: that I have a perspective. Undergoing you, I was spellbound, in awe of the mystery of the suffering that is invisible. You held me in uncomfortable thrall, delighting in your power. It was delightful. I had to undergo you. It was my love alone that held me there, allowing me to undergo the suffering that is invisible. Standing in the cool flames now with my wits about me, I notice: that my perspective is groundless. It has no purchase: the solidity that dogged me turns out to be thin air, and there is no pain in falling. I cannot be taken seriously. There is relief, but it is like dying. I am so scared, but there is no pain.

It is so strange that you had to cast me out, make me outcast: somewhere I could not recognize myself, unable to make my way back. Do you want to know me? You shall suffer deracination and homelessness. You will not know what you have lost. Then you will know me.

For life's sake I am the fool. It could have been otherwise, but it would have been the same. Does life survive life? The answer is, yes, my dear, it does so effortlessly. I love you the way you are.

I am become the great dynamo, weeping amidst my laughter. Sainthood or asylum, I am what I am. It does not make any sense, my love, but what can I tell you?

In trying to find a reason for you, I curtailed myself. You were always beyond my grasp. You hurt me so much, so that I needed to grasp you. Only because you eluded my grasping, were you beyond. It was so painful that I had to die in these flames, the words that come to me. It is so painful, this burning that frees me. There is nothing and I have given up things I never had. I no longer grasp, and you are no longer beyond. So it becomes the easiest thing. My worship was so much folly, in which I recognize absolute necessity. Such is my freedom. I am what is mysterious in life. I tried to soothe myself with explanations, but they kept me from you. I protected myself from you, and I always wanted you. I wanted you, but I was afraid. I am content with what I can never have. I knew you were the origin, and that we do not belong to ourselves. But I wanted to blame you because beyond blame there is no understanding, and I needed to save myself from the inexplicable. But you are the blameless, inexplicable flame in which I have burned. Can you hear me?

I could have killed you, but I would have rather died. You enraged me as if it had been the meaning of your existence: to force me beyond myself. You told me you loved me, but I felt and knew I was being destroyed. It's so obvious and strange, the truth of our love. You did want to destroy me, I know that now. We loved each other, yet it felt like one of us had to die. I couldn't exist because I wanted to destroy you, and it felt so awful. I loved you! And that's what you told me all the time: whispering your love while destroying me. This was treachery for which I could have murdered you. You were just doing what you had to. And so was I. What were you trying to do? You are an excruciating duality in which I have burned alive. We fought, in infinite pain, a battle to the death in which neither of us could ever die. I do not know why the pain was more bearable than this: I am that I am. It does not make very much sense, my love, but there you have it. I do not know why the pain of never dying was more bearable than this: I am that I am.

There are no implications. There are no conclusions. It is not as if being with you has given me clarity. It is not as if, being with you, certain things no longer matter. It is not as if, being with you, I have seen. I am blind and I am alive.

You're obviously the reason I'm here. All the reasons at once, refracted through whoever I am.

* * *

In another photograph you took, I am standing on one side of a fence, not far from the sea, worrying my chin with my hand. My face is sullen, as if I were afraid to take another step, without first knowing: the beginning of the universe, how it caused the present situation, and how it all ends.

111

I chose knowing, because being with you was too frightening, and I alone was given the possibility to be with you. Now I am with you, and there is nothing left to know. Because I am without cause, my love.

Who am I in your eyes? What do you see, when you see me? Was it all on purpose? Do you know what you're doing? You have made me wonder. You have broken me in the miraculous, and I don't even know what you are.

Even if, despite my better judgment, I choose to see you in all things, what made me this way? That I should choose to listen where there is nothing to hear? What made me this way? You exist, then, because I exist. It is an irrefutable delusion that I choose to share with everyone. Have I chosen you? Have you chosen me? I am so far beyond anything that makes sense. I am laughing with you, in the midst of everything and beyond it. I am an idiot, my love. I am such an idiot!

I don't know who you are anymore, and I'm afraid of losing my mind—and is this love?

I still really want to be human. It's so strange to choose death. I guess it's just the way I am. Are my concerns petty in your eyes? I thought we were done with that, my love. You're so incorrigible!

I can't believe I thought I lost you. Without you, I wouldn't be here, where I am, now. It's so obvious that I never needed to worry about losing you. Wherever I am, I am in touch with you, never outside your influence. Especially where I am now. I think that I've lost you and wonder what it was all for. And then I know: all my questions, wherever I have arrived, all the doubt: I could not have had any of this without you. So you're still here, no matter what. I couldn't be here without you, and here I am worrying that I lost you, something I wouldn't be able to do without you. It's funny, my love, it's really funny. Even when I'm crying about it.

Now, everything is the same, but different. And everything that matters is what's the same: eating and sleeping, and this afternoon, and tomorrow morning, and next week. Perhaps I am raving mad, but I've known lunatics and I don't seem to be one of them. What's different is nothing I can tell you about, and despite what I just said, what matters is that it's so very different now. Everything is different, and I can't tell you anything about it. We could talk about today and tomorrow, and everything that is the same. What else can I say? I don't know what I'm talking about: I've lost my mind. It's your fault, my love. No, it's both our faults!

Now there is nothing, and I choose to hallucinate brightly, giving myself this veil to cast aside. It will always be this way, and I will always love you.

I miss your wetness under the skirts of your white nightgown: the nights we spent lost to ourselves and each other, seeking so ardently in an oblivion that is hell compared to seeing you now. I miss the softness and gentle warmth, rising and falling, when we were gently entangled, like babies in sleep. My little dove, my dear. Like eiderdown.

Through you, I intend to find peace in my homelessness. It's not as if I'll have to do without the creature comforts. I could be wandering in great luxury, no expenses spared. You are certainly the most profligate person I ever met. Your expenditures don't even make sense.

You were always the one with the sense of humor! Now I find myself cowering in the face of my decision to speak the unspeakable. My life has led me to speak, to you, of the unspeakable. I never would have guessed that it would come to this: cowering before the unoccluded vision of my horizon. In this, I am never alone, and this is what makes everything possible: being with you, speaking with you, and living with you.

I find solace in our shared fate, which because we share it, is unpredictable. You used to terrify me into making lofty, abstract proclamations: they protected me from our shared fate, which is utterly unpredictable. I wanted to be above you, to save myself, and found out that I am you. That's the unspeakable nonsense our relationship has compelled me to articulate. I'm not blaming you. What can I tell you? I love you.

Anyway, I've spent years trying to come to terms with you, instead of reaching out my hand, living with you. I cannot express how grateful I am to share this ineffability with you, of which I still take pains to speak. It's just who I am, I suppose.

You're you. And I'm me. That's just the way it is, my love. And there's nothing we can do about it.

So, I simply want to tell you how grateful I am for the time we've spent together and for all the unforeseen things we have yet to undergo. Expressing my gratitude felt like a task whose difficulty exceeded that of conjuring the sublime. However, it's really quite easy, my love: thank you.

You can't become yourself without all the help in the world. Honestly, I still don't know who you are.

Who is leading whom, out here beyond the pale? In this poorly travelled territory, I learn how much I truly need you. You've shown me so much, and now I need to show you what I've seen. How is it possible that you don't know yet who I am? More often than not, it doesn't make any sense to me, but everything is reconciled: I love you, just the way you are.